FORCES '90

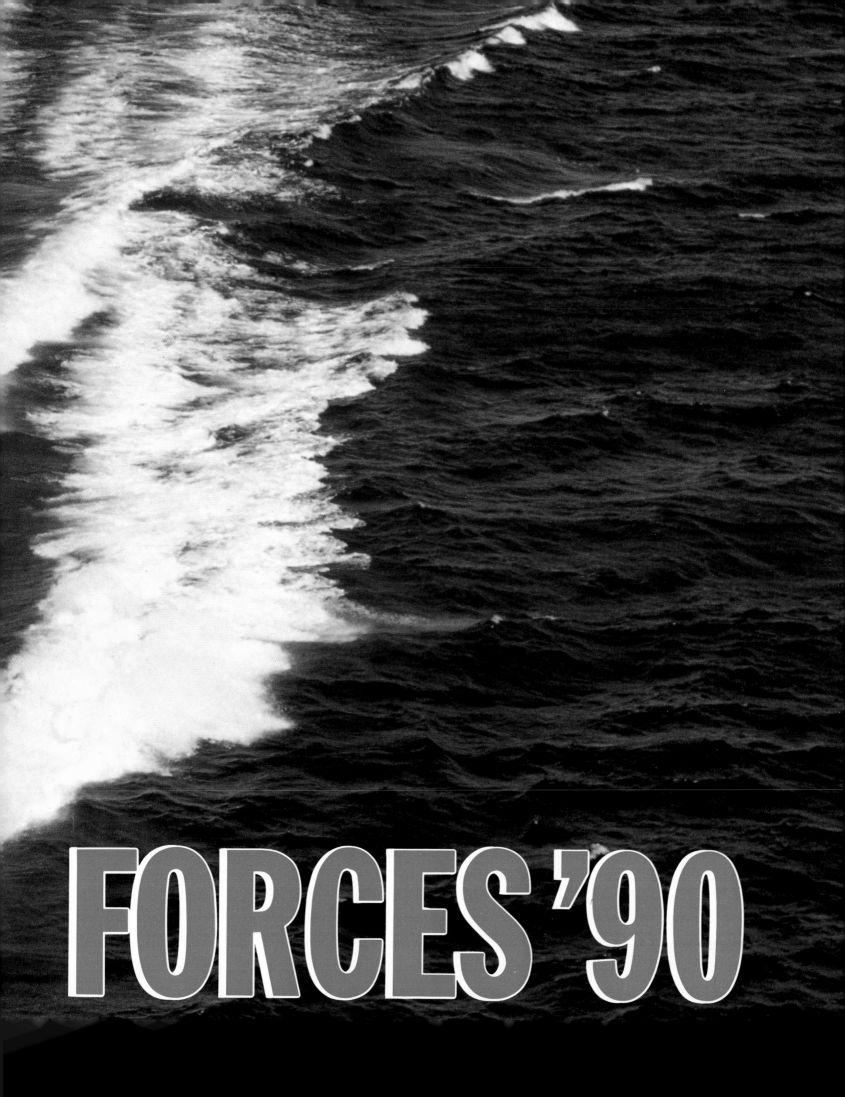

FORCES '90

Published by Marshall Cavendish Publications
58, Old Compton Street, London W1V 5PA

Editor	Lloyd Lindo
Commissioning Editor	Will Steeds
Assistant Editor	Theresa Donaghey
Art Editor	Keith Vollans
Picture Researcher	Diane Moore/MARS
Managing Editor	Sue Lyon
Consultant Editor	Mark Dartford
Production Controller	Deborah Cracknell

Typeset by Litho Link Ltd. Welshpool

CONTENTS

The A-10 Thunderbolt, designed for a close-air support, anti-armour roll. Armed with a GAU-8 30-mm cannon, it is capable of up to 70 rounds a second. The A-10 marks a radical departure from the sophisticated, all-purpose, expensive concept in aircraft design.

INTRODUCTION

The U-2 affair in the 1960s revealed the clandestine nature of aerial reconnaissance when a U-2 operated by the CIA was shot down over Russia and its pilot charged with spying. FORCES '90 surveys the history and development of reconnaissance aircraft from balloons in the sky to the launching of satellites into space.

The huge strides made in sensor technology since World War II apply to both Stealth and Reconnaissance programmes. The emergence of the first stealth bomber, the US B-2, focuses attention on this most sophisticated and expensive form of military hardware.

The Pacific Basin – backyard of two of the world's superpowers – reverberates with the consequences of the Vietnam War and the clamour of nations jostling for position on the economic, military and political stage. We review the changing scenario in this strategically important region.

In the area of conflict, the ill-fated invasion of Afghanistan by Russia is spotlighted, with the motivation for and after-effects of the war being considered.

The Royal Artillery is this year's featured regiment. There is also a feature on the 'wasps' of the sea – Fast Patrol Boats – and a behind-the-scenes look at Western officer training. As always, FORCES concludes its fascinating insights with the diary – a review of the year's events and activities.

Tiananmen Square – scene of the students' protests that led up to the massacre, when soldiers were ordered to open fire on the crowds and charge them with tanks.

Chapter 1

AIR WAR:
Aerial Reconnaissance

In a future war it would be suicidal to send reconnaissance aircraft across hostile heartlands unless they were either 'stealth' designs or, alternatively, extremely small Remotely Piloted Vehicles (RPVs). Invaluable support to the high-tech intelligence gatherers on land, at sea, in the sky and in space can be provided by relatively low-tech methods of aerial reconnaissance, using various forms of conventional film camera, video cameras, IR sensors and radars, all studying hostile territory from relatively close range.

Crew of an RF-4C Phantom adopt a 'hands clear' posture during last-minute checks by ground crew shortly before take-off. The RF-4C brought back pre- and post-strike reconnaissance photographs of targets in some of the most heavily defended regions of Vietnam.

On August 27 1783 Prof J A C Charles launched his first unmanned hydrogen balloon in Paris. Someone said 'Very interesting, but what use is it?' The great American Benjamin Franklin growled back 'What use is a new-born baby?' The story may not be true, but a use appeared quite soon. Following experiments at Meudon in April 1794 the French Army formed a 'compagnie des Aérostiers', and on June 26 1794 Capt J M J Coutelle watched the entire Battle of Fleurus from about 1,000 ft (305 m). He was the only member of Gen Jourdan's Army of the Moselle not on the ground, and an official history says 'the information which he signalled to Jourdan proved to be a material factor in the far-reaching victory which the French forces gained over the Allies . . .'

Coutelle's balloon was captive, linked to the ground by a rope. Similar captive balloons were used in the American Civil War and Boer War, and many thousands were used by various participants in World War I, by which time the balloons shared the sky with aircraft. Despite being armed with incendiary Le Prieur rockets and machine guns firing incendiary ammunition, aircraft as a means of shooting down balloons were considered both difficult and hazardous.

Early beginnings

Reconnaissance aeroplanes first appeared in October 1911 when Italian Capt Piazza flew his Blériot XI over Turkish troops for a full hour between Tripoli and Azizia. He wrote down or sketched everything of interest. The same officer scored another 'first' on February 24 1912 when he photographed the enemy with a bulky plate camera. On April 19 1912 Cmdt Sulsi used a cine camera over the Turkish forces, aiming it from airship P3. Thus, the methods that were to remain standard for aerial reconnaissance for 40 years were already in use before the start of World War I.

At the start of World War I by far the most important British military aircraft was the BE2 biplane. It was made in enormous quantities in several versions, but all shared the same basic characteristics of low performance, an inability to deploy effective firepower and supreme natural stability.

The designer, Geoffrey de Havilland, deliberately made the BE stable so that pilot and observer could concentrate on watching the enemy, making notes and taking photographs. By summer 1915 agile Fokker fighters began to hack down the BEs in droves, because the highly stable biplanes simply could not be manoeuvred out of the streams of bullets.

Equally serious at first was that most observers – crew members specifically tasked with surveillance of the enemy – were totally inexperienced and often untrained, and field commanders began to doubt their reports. Gradually the aircraft, the cameras and the observers began to improve.

The first British camera specially designed for aerial use, the Thornton-Pickard Type A, was a great improvement on all that had gone before, but the observer – scared, keyed up with nervous tension, probably airsick and certainly suffering in the cold – had to lean over the side of the lurching cockpit, with neither parachute nor restraining harness, and with frozen, gloved fingers work the controls.

This battle scene painted on a snuff box lid depicts the Battle of Fleurus in Belgium in 1794 between the French revolutionary army and the Austrians. It was at this battle that a hydrogen balloon, linked to the ground by a rope, was used for aerial reconnaissance. The French, led by Marshal Jourdan, were victorious. This victory was attributable in large measure to the information passed on by Capt J M J Coutelle from his 1,000 ft (305 m) vantage point. It was the first use of aerial reconnaissance.

Between the Wars

Developments in aerial reconnaissance between the World Wars were unimpressive and patchy. The greatest progress was made in the cameras and film. Cameras improved optically, giving fine definition from heights which by 1939 could exceed 30,000 ft (9,140 m). This was paralleled by vastly improved film stock sensitive to various wavelengths, including infra-red.

The cameras were developed so that they could be mounted away from the crew, totally remotely controlled and heated so that even in the freezing stratosphere they would work properly, with clear lenses. Not least, the film magazines were designed so that, after each sortie, ground crew could remove the film in seconds and rush it to the processing section.

Britain's RAF and the French Armée de l'Air had little idea how such cameras should be used, and put them in a hodge-podge of regular squadron aircraft. In the USA, several technical developments were made. One of them was an installation of three large cameras in a fan array to give horizon-to-horizon coverage, or coverage of any lesser strip of ground.

The Army, however, thought of airpower as an adjunct to the land battle – as did the Soviet Union – and it called its reconnaissance aircraft 'observation airplanes'. This made everyone think in terms of hand-held cameras and writing on a pad.

Hitler's Luftwaffe had everything going for it, including a lack of hidebound tradition, the world's best optical industry and the ability to specify new aircraft designed for the job. Rightly, the Luftwaffe saw the need for two distinct aircraft classes. The role of short-range tactical reconnaissance and army co-operation aircraft was met

Above: German troops during World War I manoeuvring an observation balloon before its ascent to begin one of many reconnaissance missions.

by the Hs 126 and later the Fw 189, its crew almost surrounded by a transparent canopy. The role of long-range strategic reconnaissance aircraft was never fully met, but resulted in such advanced aircraft as the Hs 130 and Ju 86R. These had highly supercharged engines, pressurized cockpits and wings of enormous span, for long missions at heights up to 51,000 ft (15,550 m).

Remarkably, a single civilian played a key role in helping Britain understand what air reconnaissance was all about. Australian Sidney Cotton spent the final year of peace making cloak-and-dagger flights over Germany and the Middle East, taking pictures of fantastic quality showing all the most sensitive objectives. No RAF or Fleet Air Arm unit could match his results.

After the outbreak of World War II, Cotton formed a small RAF unit from which grew a vast organization called PRU (Photographic Reconnaissance Unit). This put excellent cameras looking down from high-speed aircraft, such as special versions of Spitfire and Mosquito, which photographed every requested target in the European theatre from around 35,000 ft (10,670 m). PRU Spitfires, and Mustang Is of Army Co-operation Command, also flew missions at tree-top height, with cameras looking sideways.

Reconnaissance can only obtain the evidence; if the evidence is misinterpreted it is useless. An essential adjunct to the PRU was the PIU, the Photographic Interpretation Unit. Long experience made the inter-

Left: The make-shift camera port in a World War II aircraft. The need to wear padded gloves in the cold air would have hindered the camera operator.

preters extremely skilled. They had to be aware of technical developments so they could search for previously unknown objects.

For example, a photograph of the Luftwaffe test airfield at Rechlin showed the twin streaks in the grass left by the jets of a prototype Me 262. And when a photograph of the rocketry research establishment at Peenemünde showed what looked like a tiny aeroplane, interpreter Constance Babington-Smith of the WAAF showed that it was the Fi 103 flying bomb, popularly called a V1 or Doodlebug.

When another Peenemünde picture showed an A4 (V2) rocket on its trailer, the professional interpreters pointed out what it was but the experts refused to believe the evidence. The most senior man of all, Professor Lindemann (later Lord Cherwell) utterly rejected the idea of a rocket. When asked for an alternative explanation he said 'a barrage balloon', and stuck to his guns until rockets were falling on London.

Limiting factor

The achievements depend crucially on the aircraft available. Reconnaissance missions try to avoid combat, and indeed are often flown by unarmed aircraft. For their safe return they rely on superior performance, notably in height and speed. From the end of the Battle of Britain in the autumn of 1940 the Luftwaffe no longer had an edge in speed or height over RAF fighters defending Britain, and with long warning time given by radar it became perilous to attempt to fly over the British Isles by day.

The German photographic coverage of its close and dangerous enemy was thus virtually non-existent. The build-up of the RAF, the US 8th and 9th Air Forces, the Allied navies and all the plans for the invasion of Festung Europa on June 6 1944 went unrecorded.

Suddenly, in late September 1944, a specially formed Luftwaffe unit, the Sonderkommando Götz, began sending Ar 234B-1 reconnaissance aircraft to photograph British ports from London to Yarmouth, to watch for an Allied invasion of The Netherlands. They brought back beautiful pictures with no problems, entirely because the Arado was a high-speed, high-altitude jet.

Later the Sonderkommando Sommer was activated with just three Ar 234Bs at Udine, and immediately began supplying perfect coverage of the Italian front. Marshal Kesselring's command in that theatre had had virtually zero air-reconnaissance input for two years previously, but the Arados arrived too late.

Technology comes of age

At the end of World War II the world was at the dawn of the Jet Age and the Nuclear Age, both of which had repercussions on aerial reconnaissance. It had also gone some way beyond the dawn of Electronic Warfare (EW), one branch of which is concerned with the family of 'int' (intelligence) technologies, such as Rint, Sigint, Elint and Comint. What might be termed legitimate aerial reconnaissance is related to these technologies and it was simultaneously transformed.

Jet aircraft could carry cameras almost twice as high and more than twice as fast as before, and developments in various laboratories led to the introduction of new sensors. Almost every new sensor made use of fresh parts of the electromagnetic spectrum.

Reconnaissance aircraft began to use radars, TV and

other electro-optical (EO) wavelengths, and infra-red (IR). The sole publicly known exception to this was a totally different range of sensors developed for a specific purpose during the Vietnam War.

By 1945, reconnaissance aircraft had become grouped into three distinct categories. The largest, used for long-range strategic missions against enemy heartlands, were versions of bombers. The fastest, used for tactical missions over battlefields and up to perhaps 200 miles (320 km) into enemy territory, often at very low level, were versions of fighters.

The third category were observation and army co-operation aircraft, operating always at low level to get an overview of a land battle. These were low-performance fixed-wing lightplanes and, later, scout helicopters. The three categories could hardly be more different.

The first category tended merely to replace bombs by cameras. At first there was little need to modify the basic aircraft. In the years after 1945, jet propulsion transformed the performance of aircraft so that, for a time, the balance appeared to favour the bomber rather than the fighter. Bombers needed all the speed and over-target height they could reach, and these were precisely the qualities needed by the strategic reconnaissance aircraft.

The multi-role option
Generally, there were no major difficulties in carrying cameras instead of bombs, although some bombers designed to carry a single nuclear weapon had smaller weapons bays than traditional bombers. A further factor is that, especially in the aftermath of a major war when defence funding is low, air forces prefer to use aircraft

Below: A Supermarine Spitfire (FR Mk XVIII) of the RAF's Photographic Reconnaissance Unit with a camera port in the fuselage.

Above: Reconnaissance information, such as the presence of an underwater sand bank off Port-en-Bessin, proved invaluable to Allied forces in 1944.

for more than one purpose. So, instead of buying one aircraft as a bomber and a second of the same type for reconnaissance, most air forces opted for a dual role bomber/reconnaissance aircraft.

Such aircraft had been common in the 1930s, but in the 1950s the engineering was more difficult. The first photo-reconnaissance (PR) versions of the ubiquitous British Canberra, the PR3 and PR7, merely had cameras fitted into the bomb bay. The installations and airframe changes were permanent, and there was no optically flat bomb-aiming panel in the transparent nosecap. These were dedicated reconnaissance aircraft, unable to fulfil a dual role.

With the bigger Valiant, however, the RAF tried harder. The first batches were pure bombers. Next came the Valiant B(PR)1, able to fly bombing or photo-reconnaissance missions. For even greater versatility Vickers produced the Valiant B(PR)K1, able to serve as bomber, photo-recon aircraft or as refuelling tanker.

Such versatility was not sought for the later Victor. As originally built, all Victors were pure bombers except for a batch of nine strategic reconnaissance Victor SR2s. In a few documents they are referred to as B(SR)2, but they never had capability as bombers.

Strategic thinking
These special Victors show the thinking of the RAF on strategic reconnaissance in the mid-1960s. The ability to carry the Blue Steel cruise missile was eliminated, and part of the sealed bomb bay was occupied by two tanks each holding 8,000 lb (3,600 kg) of fuel. The rest of the space was given over to 'the largest reconnaissance camera crate ever used by a Western air force'.

The most significant feature was that, although there were other options, in practice every sensor was a conventional film camera. These were backed up by 108 large (3,000,000 candlepower) photoflashes. As in World War II, these were dropped accurately in night missions and the camera shutter timed to open immediately before the flash illuminated the scene.

The H₂S mapping radar was retained but locked to look sideways and linked with advanced radar mapping and display processors. It was said at the time (about October 1965) that a single SR2 'could photograph every ship in the Mediterranean in a six-hour sortie'.

Shortsightedly, the RAF converted all surviving Victors as air-refuelling tankers. In April 1982, following Argentina's invasion of the Falklands, there was deep concern at the need to mount military operations in one of the most remote places on Earth. In a matter of days, new equipment was fitted into Victor K2 tankers, including Carousel IV inertial navigation systems and receivers for the Omega global electronic navigation aid. Then on April 20 a Victor equipped with H₂S radar and captained by S/L John Elliott made a sortie of over 7,000 miles (11,300 km) – at the time a world record for any air combat mission – lasting 14 hours and 45 minutes, to make a reconnaissance of the sea area north of South Georgia.

In the USA several outstanding dedicated reconnaissance prototypes were flown immediately after World War II, including the Hughes XF-11, Republic XF-12 and Northrop XF-15, but none was adopted. But the USAAF (from 1947 the USAF) continued to use special versions of fighters and bombers, such as the RF-80, RF-84, RB-36 and RB-47.

When the eight-jet YB-52 made its first flight in April 1952 plans went ahead for an RB-52B version able to fly either strategic bombing or reconnaissance missions. The distinguishing feature of this version was that the capacious weapons bay was designed to accept either bombs or a tight-fitting pressurized container accommodating a two-man crew and various arrangements of cameras or electronic sensors. This was to see only limited service with Strategic Air Command, and the various RB-58A models of the Convair Hustler supersonic bomber did not go into service at all.

On the other hand the US Navy ordered 30 Douglas A3D-2P Skywarriors (later redesignated RA-3B) and these saw much active service with two squadrons, VAP-61 and -62. These units provided detached flights for global deployment aboard carriers of the Atlantic or Pacific Fleets. These aircraft were major rebuilds from the original attack version. The whole fuselage was pressurized, and in the former weapons-bay area was accommodation for two reconnaissance specialists and up to 12 vertical and oblique cameras.

A complementary and related version was the A3D-2Q (later EA-3B), in which the mid-fuselage provided accommodation for four electronic-warfare specialists and equipment for electronic reconnaissance.

To a considerable degree the replacement for the RA-3B was the RA-5C Vigilante. Designed as an extremely advanced carrier-based supersonic bomber, the Vigilante saw only brief service in that role. The upgraded RA-5C reconnaissance version, however, was the US Navy's standard long-range reconnaissance platform for over 20 years from 1964.

Unlike the RA-3B, no specialist crew members were necessary for the RA-5C. Instead, the underside of the fuselage was occupied by an impressive array of vertical, oblique and split-image cameras, and a canoe fairing along the belly housed the antenna of a Side-Looking Airborne Radar (SLAR). This radar sends out a narrow beam which 'paints' the ground to one side (sometimes both) of the aircraft. Because of the aircraft's forwards motion, each sweep of the beam sees a different strip of ground. The resulting signals are assembled to form a continuous photographic print-out, with no overlaps and no gaps.

How far the SLAR can see depends on several factors, notably how high the aircraft is flying. During the Vietnam War the RA-5C carried out all the Navy's strategic reconnaissance in that theatre. One true story is that, following measurement by photo interpreters of a Vigilante's recon pictures, an American football ground was carefully measured and found to be (incorrectly) 100.1 yards long. The Vigilante had recorded the error from an oblique range of 60 miles (96.6 km).

In parallel with the Vigilante worked the Vought RF-8A Crusader (later rebuilt to RF-8G standard). This was a typical reconnaissance aircraft based on a supersonic fighter, with the guns in the forward

Left: The Vigilante was the US Navy's standard long-range reconnaissance aircraft for over 20 years from 1964. It was equipped with vertical, oblique and split-image cameras, plus a Side-Looking Airborne Radar (SLAR).

Above: The RF-8G Crusader reconnaissance aircraft worked in parallel with the Vigilante. Five cameras replaced the guns in the forward fuselage.

fuselage replaced by five cameras. Like other aircraft in this class the Crusaders could fly very high or very low, but were limited by their combat radius of well under 500 miles (800 km). At high altitude, however, the photo Crusader could appear impressive, as when on July 16 1957 Marine John Glenn (later Astronaut and Senator) made a photographic record from Los Angeles to New York in under 3 h 23 min, which (despite air refuelling) represented an average speed at the height he was flying of well over Mach 1.

Throughout the world similar dedicated reconnaissance aircraft derived from fighters were (and still are) used in large numbers. Most were simply fitted with cameras in place of guns or other equipment, but when in 1962 the USAF decided to do the unheard-of and adopt a Navy aircraft, the F-4 Phantom II, it decided at the same time to procure a reconnaissance version that would break new ground. The result was the RF-4C, first delivered to Tactical Air Command in 1965.

New sensors

The RF-4C was able to carry not only cameras but also SLAR (never before fitted to a fighter-type aircraft), an infra-red linescan (IRLS) and several other devices, as well as photo cartridges and a high frequency (HF) radio with suppressed antennas in the fin and global range. The IRLS was perhaps the most important of all the completely new sensors developed since 1945. It comprises an optical system which focuses IR (heat) radiation from the ground on to an array of sensitive detectors, the output signals then being processed to generate a picture. This picture looks very much like any other monochrome (black-and-white) photo except that it records differences in temperature. Usually, warmer areas are whiter and colder areas blacker, but this sensing can be reversed if necessary.

Using IR instead of visible light to form an image has interesting advantages. It can show which chimney of a power station is hot. It can show if the engine of a truck is running. It can show which aircraft in a flightline has just landed after a high-altitude sortie, its wings still housing fuel at perhaps −55°C. It can show the spot where a truck or aircraft was recently parked. A single linescan image of a Soviet warship once showed over 100 points of interest, most of them invisible to a normal optical camera.

In addition to new sensors, reconnaissance aircraft were seen to be in increasing peril except at either very low or very high altitudes. The very low aircraft continued to include fast jets and slow piston-engined aircraft. In the Korean War (1950-53) T-6 Texan (Harvard) trainers joined with even less powerful two-seaters, notably the Cessna L-19 (later 0-1) Bird Dog, in flying what at the time were called tactical co-ordinator missions, and in Vietnam were called Forward Air Control (FAC) missions. These represented reconnaissance at the closest and most basic level. Defying all fire from the ground, these small unarmed and unarmoured aircraft would investigate everywhere that hostile troops could hide.

Having found something, they would call up attack aircraft and either mark the spot with a smoke bomb or rocket or simply describe the location by radio. It was said that the value of such on-the-spot reconnaissance was enormous, but in due course individual soldiers have been armed with portable Surface-to-Air Missiles (SAMs), making such close surveillance almost certainly suicidal.

At the other end of the height scale came special versions of established reconnaissance aircraft, as well as aircraft designed from the outset for ultra-high flying. The established recon category included variants of the

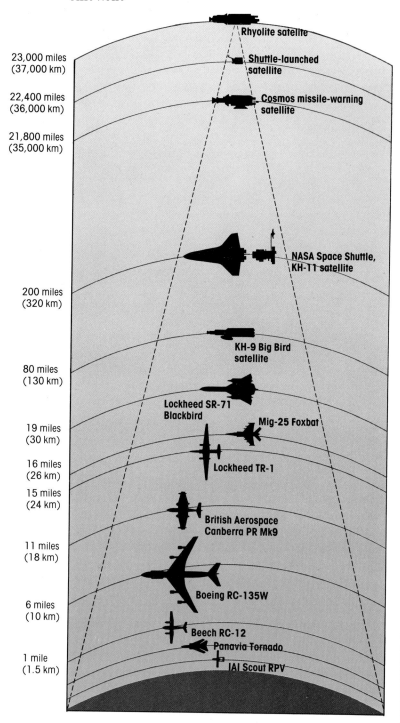

23,000 miles
(37,000 km)

Rhyolite satellite

Shuttle-launched
satellite

22,400 miles
(36,000 km)

Cosmos missile-warning
satellite

21,800 miles
(35,000 km)

200 miles
(320 km)

NASA Space Shuttle,
KH-11 satellite

KH-9 Big Bird
satellite

80 miles
(130 km)

Lockheed SR-71
Blackbird

Mig-25 Foxbat

19 miles
(30 km)

16 miles
(26 km)

Lockheed TR-1

15 miles
(24 km)

British Aerospace
Canberra PR Mk9

11 miles
(18 km)

Boeing RC-135W

6 miles
(10 km)

Beech RC-12

Panavia Tornado

1 mile
(1.5 km)

IAI Scout RPV

Above: The operational altitudes of reconnaissance
vehicles range from tree-top height, for remotely piloted
vehicles and low-flying aircraft, to the satellite realms
22,000 miles above the Earth.

Canberra. The RAF set its sights quite low; the PR9
version (first delivered in early 1960) featured more
powerful engines and an 8.9 per cent increase in wing
area, to give a modest increase in operating altitude. By
contrast, the USAF's B-57 version was modified by
General Dynamics into the RB-57F version with three
times the power and double the wingspan.

Ultra-high flying

Even this amazing aircraft paled into insignificance
beside the aircraft specially built to meet a USAF's MX-

2147 programme which in 1953 called for a reconnaissance aircraft to make the maximum use of new
engines, long-span wings and other features to fly
higher than any previous aircraft.

Submissions were made by Bell, Fairchild and
Martin. Bell was named winner, and Martin delivered
RB-57Ds as stop-gap interim aircraft, but the final
winner was a dark horse from Lockheed, born in total
secrecy and destined to a life of intrigue, suddenly
punctuated by the startling news on May 1 1960 that a
Lockheed U-2 had been shot down by SAMs near
Sverdlovsk, in the heart of the Soviet Union. The
secret was out.

For years, U-2s operated by the US Central Intelligence Agency (not by any branch of the armed forces)
had been methodically 'overflying' the Soviet Union and
any other place of interest to the United States, at
altitudes exceeding 75,000 ft (22,900 m). Here they
were almost invisible – unless water vapour from
the jet froze to leave a contrail – and certainly
uninterceptable (it was thought).

The U-2s carried various sensors, at first almost
exclusively cameras of which the specially designed
Type B was the most important. Its side-sweeping
lens, folded optics and bulk film magazine enabled it to
bring back film of fabulous clarity over a strip length of
1,000 miles (1,600 km) or more.

Sverdlovsk caused no more than a hiccup in the
programme, and the U-2 was developed through a
multitude of versions, carrying often fantastic sensors,
leading up to the TR-1. But by the late 1950s it
appeared that mere altitude was no longer enough to
confer immunity from interception. There appeared to
be two solutions. One was to combine extreme altitude
with extreme speed. The other, and probably harder,
was to make aircraft essentially undetectable.

Into space

There was also by this time a third solution. From the
launch of Sputnik I on October 4 1957 it had been
obvious that artificial satellites of Earth could be
developed to fulfil reconnaissance roles. As early as
April 1 1960 a Thor-Able rocket launched a satellite
called TIROS 1 (from Television and Infra-Red Observation Satellite). It was followed on May 24 1960 by the
first MIDAS (MIssile Defense Alarm System), carrying
sensitive IR detectors to pinpoint the launch of ballistic
missiles from a distance of several hundred miles.

On January 31 1961 the USAF followed with the first
SAMOS (Satellite And Missile Observation System),
the first Western reconnaissance satellite to use
conventional photography. The SAMOS was the first of
many satellites, notably including the prolific Discoverer
series, to eject capsules containing exposed film and
other records such as magnetic tape Elint data.

After entering the atmosphere the capsules deployed
a parachute, and then were snatched in mid-air by a
C-130 Hercules transport. At first a trapeze arrange-

ment was used, deployed from the rear cargo doors. Later the nose-mouthed Fulton recovery gear came into use, with long pivoted arms like the jaws of an insect. Subsequently, recon satellites of both the USA and Soviet Union have reached a remarkable degree of refinement.

Prime contractor for the biggest USAF spy satellites is Lockheed. The same company produced both the first 'undetectable' aircraft and the 'high and fast' aircraft. The latter first flew on April 26 1962, in the form of the A-12, first of a family of Blackbird aircraft able to cruise at 3.2 times the speed of sound. A year later the A-12 was tested as launch vehicle for the D-21 reconnaissance drone, a large ramjet-propelled vehicle able to cruise at Mach 4. Several D-21s were later flown from B-52 launch aircraft.

Much more successful was the basic Blackbird, which on 22 December 1964 first flew in SR-71A form. The SR-71A has for 25 years flown all over the world as the USAF's chief manned clandestine reconnaissance aircraft, carrying the biggest and most sophisticated cameras in the sky, and various other sensors.

The first 'undetectable' aircraft were small tactical machines modified by Lockheed from Schweizer sailplanes. The need in Vietnam was for a craft that could keep watch from close range on Viet Cong infiltrating at night. Tests with the rebuilt sailplanes, fitted with specially adapted engine/propeller systems, led to the YO-3A, called 'The Quiet One'. This carried a crew of one or two plus IR, Elint or cameras. When passing overhead at 100 ft (30 m) it was said to be virtually silent, making a noise 'like distant leaves in the breeze'. This was to lead to today's Stealth aircraft.

Reconnaissance today

The penetration of hostile territory – at any height, from tree-top to satellite orbit – seems to become more fraught with danger every week. However, some of today's systems, ranging from satellites to airships and microlights, have never been tested in war; and an objective observer might conclude that they were going to need a large element of luck.

The methods used depend critically upon the kind of conflict and the sophistication and power of the enemy. As the obvious leader of the so-called Western world, both politically and technically, the USA has for 45 years kept at least one eye on the Soviet Union, but has actually had to fight major wars only in Korea and Vietnam. It won neither and, moreover, these conflicts were against relatively primitive ground forces.

In Vietnam, helicopters could fly low over areas where the VC were suspected, using a 'people sniffer' sensitive to human perspiration chemicals to find them. Other aircraft would drop various forms of sensors beside the Ho Chi Minh trails to detect trucks by their atmospheric noise and ground vibrations. To try to use such methods against a major power would be futile.

Today the world's major air forces undertake reconnaissance of many contrasting kinds. The type that has changed least in the past 20, or even 50, years is the long-range maritime patrol, with particular interest in the presence and location of hostile surface fleets and submarines. On the surface the obvious sensor is radar, with an antenna designed to sweep the horizon ahead.

Below: The Electronic RV-1D Mohawk reconnaissance aircraft of the US Army Intelligence Battalion.

Grumman OV-1 Mohawk

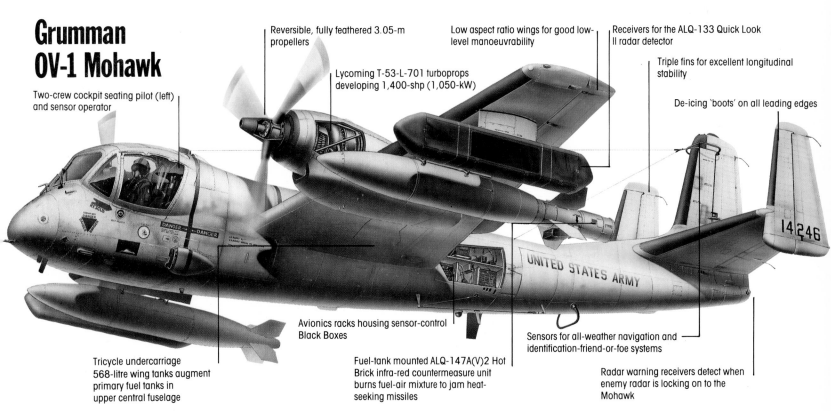

Two-crew cockpit seating pilot (left) and sensor operator

Reversible, fully feathered 3.05-m propellers

Lycoming T-53-L-701 turboprops developing 1,400-shp (1,050-kW)

Low aspect ratio wings for good low-level manoeuvrability

Receivers for the ALQ-133 Quick Look II radar detector

Triple fins for excellent longitudinal stability

De-icing 'boots' on all leading edges

Tricycle undercarriage 568-litre wing tanks augment primary fuel tanks in upper central fuselage

Avionics racks housing sensor-control Black Boxes

Fuel-tank mounted ALQ-147A(V)2 Hot Brick infra-red countermeasure unit burns fuel-air mixture to jam heat-seeking missiles

Sensors for all-weather navigation and identification-friend-or-foe systems

Radar warning receivers detect when enemy radar is locking on to the Mohawk

In actual warfare it would be rash to alert hostile ESM systems in this way, so it might be better to use a sensitive Forward-Looking IR (FLIR) sensor, which is passive and undetectable.

Against submarines, the chief sensors continue to be acoustic ones, using either sonobuoys dropped into the ocean or dipping (dunking) sonar. These devices use the ability of sound waves to travel great distances through seawater. The latest designs can emit directional beams, like radar, and their performance is more than 1,000 times better than in 1945. Another important ASW method is Magnetic Anomaly Detection (MAD), which detects and measures the small distortion of the terrestrial magnetic field caused by a submarine.

Air forces today are much less willing to 'overfly' unfriendly territory than they were up until the beginning of the 1980s. A perceived thawing of the Cold War and a greater wish not to provoke crises are partly the reason, but the greatest discouragement is that aircraft that do so are unlikely to return. Even the SR-71s of the USAF's 9th Strategic Reconnaissance Wing have progressively curtailed their activities; a mission by them is now a rare event. The precise work of this unit – an element of Strategic Air Command – has always been highly classified, but there is no doubt that in the past it has been used to overfly all but the most sensitive target areas. Today it is extremely doubtful that it crosses any frontier without permission.

Terrain mapping

The only 'replacement' for the SR-71 is the reconnaissance satellite. Lockheed launched the Big Bird family in June 1971. These impressive platforms are 49 ft (15 m) long, typically weigh 28,660 lb (13,000 kg) and carry a SLAR as well as an Eastman Kodak survey camera and a Perkin-Elmer camera for high-resolution study of small areas. From 1976, Big Birds were backed up by KH-11 satellites weighing typically 20,100 lb (9,100 kg) and remaining on station two years rather than Big Bird's six months.

The KH-11s output digital data gives information in different visual colours plus IR, UV and radar with extraordinary definition. A particularly important task of KH-11s and other satellites during the 1980s has been to make extremely accurate and detailed maps of the terrain in large areas of potentially hostile countries. This is because the chief method of navigation of future attack aircraft and cruise missiles will be TERCOM (Terrain Contour Matching) or some other terrain-referenced system which senses and follows the land contours under the flight path.

In terms of numbers, the Soviet recon satellites far outnumber those of the United States. The Cosmos series alone numbers more than 2,000.

The policy of avoiding overflights has thrown greater emphasis on surveillance from aircraft flying along frontiers. Since 1980 the NATO nations have addressed this problem with unparalleled vigour. The result is a series of air platforms covering the whole range of usable heights, looking into Warsaw Pact territory with a wide range of sensors.

At the top end of the altitude band is the Lockheed TR-1, today's successor to the clandestine U-2. The TR-1A is outwardly almost identical to the U-2R, a greatly enlarged, black-painted U-2 version which certainly has made clandestine missions, mainly in the

Elint role. By contrast, the TR-1A appears to be operated in a completely open manner, standing off at a height of 70,000 ft (21,300 m) and flying the length of (say) the frontier between East and West Germany.

Its main sensor is a large Advanced Synthetic-Aperture Radar System (ASARS). An SAR behaves as if it had an antenna hundreds of feet long, and so can generate images with high definition, at least as good as reconnaissance photographs. The difference is that the radar can look obliquely out to a great distance yet produce an image which appears to be viewed from directly above. The ASARS can look 35 miles (56 km) into unfriendly territory. Additional sensors can be carried in the fuselage and in large pods on the wings. The USAF has funded 28 TR-1As, about 20 of which have been delivered.

The equivalent RAF aircraft is a rebuild of the Canberra PR9. With the minimum of publicity, five of

Left: The RF-4C reconnaissance variant of the McDonnell Douglas Phantom at take-off. The Phantom is the best reconnaissance platform available to NATO. Pre-mission checks (above) include loading cameras with film and electronic sensors with magnetic tape. Other pre-flight checks are made during taxiing.

these aircraft have been returned to Shorts of Belfast – which manufactured them 30 years previously – for complete refurbishment and the installation of a radar similar to ASARS but called Airborne STand-Off Radar (ASTOR). Apparently, there are two competing radars, one by GEC Avionics having already been tested in a Canberra.

As a cheaper alternative, a low-level option exists in which a completely different form of ASTOR made by Ferranti would be mounted in the nose of a small twin-turboprop Defender. Flight trials began in 1984, when the radar was called CASTOR, the C standing for Corps because the data would be relayed to army groups at that high level. In 1989 the Defender was expected to be testing a third radar option, the Thorn EMI Skymaster. What appears to be uncertain is whether the detailed information needed by the land forces can be gained over the desired range from a Defender unable to climb above 23,000 ft (7,000 m).

Down the height scale to about 10,000 ft (3,000 m), 1995 could see the French Orchidée system coming into service to co-ordinate all elements of the French (and probably other) ground forces. Orchidée is French for orchid, but it is also an acronym derived from the French for 'coherent radar for investigating the enemy'. Carried beneath a Super Puma II helicopter, Orchidée is an advanced Doppler radar capable of detailed surveillance to a depth of 62 miles (100 km) inside hostile territory while the helicopter stands off at 10,000 ft (3,000 m) and a distance of 31 miles (50 km) inside its own territory. What has yet to be explained is how these aircraft are expected to survive in wartime, because all will be within easy SAM range.

External pods

One class of aircraft specifically designed to survive in the face of the enemy are the fast jets, variously known as 'fighters' or 'attack aircraft'. Aircraft in this category, notably F-4C/D/E Phantoms, served in the Vietnam War in the FAC role – a dangerous and demanding duty. Since 1960, an increasing proportion of such aircraft have been equipped to carry reconnaissance sensors packaged into an external pod. At first such pods housed only optical cameras, some forward oblique, some vertical or in a fan, and probably one rotating or swinging about a longitudinal axis to give horizon-to-horizon coverage. By 1965, IR linescan was beginning to appear; indeed the Swedish Red Baron pod (1970) carried nothing else.

This ability to package sensors either into a fuselage bay or into an external pod has led to some services, such as the RAF and Fleet Air Arm, no longer having any dedicated reconnaissance aircraft (at least until the five Canberra PR9s are redelivered). For example, the Harrier GR3 can carry a small camera pod externally, the Harrier GR5 can have a FLIR in the nose, and the Tornado GR1 can have a side-looking IR and an IR linescan. Pilots and crews may have to perform air

combat, attack and recon duties in one mission, so they must be versatile and skilled in all three roles.

In complete contrast, the West German Luftwaffe uses the Tornado ECR (Electronic Combat and Reconnaissance), which is dedicated to these missions and has sensors occupying the fuselage bays which in the GR1 house the guns and ammunition. The largest ECR sensor is an Emitter Locator System (ELS), which detects hostile ground-based emissions and, using a precision direction-finding system, pinpoints and records their source. Other sensors include a FLIR and an IR linescan, plus comprehensive processing, storage, display and transmission systems.

Tornados have also flown with external multisensor pods, and one has been evaluated in a search for the optimum reconnaissance version of the F-16. The Royal Netherlands AF has been using the F-16A(R) since 1983, but General Dynamics has itself funded what it calls the F-16 Recce project, aimed at producing the best compromise. Much flying has been done with a large semi-conformal pod (which contours the fuselage) packed with advanced EO and IR sensors, plus an imagery management system, to confer all-weather day and night capability at all speeds and altitudes, with all imagery available at ground stations very close to real time. This pod is 14 ft 5 in (4.39 m) long and weighs about 1,200 lb (550 kg), but it is stressed to the same 9 g manoeuvre limit as the F-16.

Stealth technology

Although the basic idea goes back to before 1914 (with aircraft covered with material such as Cellophane instead of fabric) it is only since the Vietnam War that the United States has developed 'low observable' or 'stealth' aircraft. The Lockheed YO-3A addressed only the question of noise, whereas the stealth concept tries to solve the far more difficult problems of minimizing visual appearance, IR emission and Radar Cross Section (RCS). Following very successful tests with small XST (experimental stealth technology) aircraft from 1977, Lockheed developed the F-117A, 55 of which were delivered to the USAF.

Despite its fighter designation the F-117A is designed for two missions: reconnaissance and strike. Almost all details of how it is used remain classified, but its ability to approach very close to enemy defences without being detected clearly enables it to fly reconnaissance missions that for other aircraft would be suicidal. Another name for the programme was CSIRS (from Covert Survivable In-weather Reconnaissance Strike), emphasizing its ability to fly missions in bad weather and to survive in conditions that would be deadly for more 'visible' aircraft.

No twin-jet aircraft can ever be silent, and perhaps the most difficult task of all is to reduce the giant IR emission from the engines until it is virtually undetectable. Few people know whether the RCS of this pioneer aircraft is so low that it can fly with impunity across hostile defences at heights between, say, 10,000 and 40,000 ft (3,000 and 12,000 m), or whether the preferred method is to keep very low as is the case with stridently observable aircraft.

Almost stealth-like is the category of aircraft which

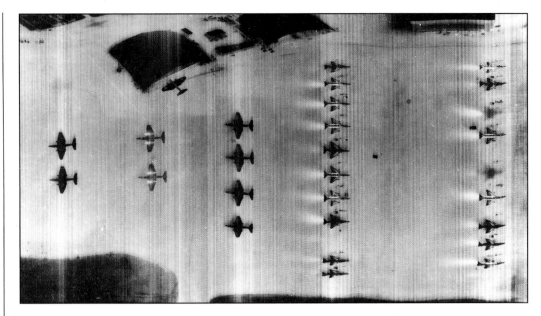

Left: This example of aerial reconnaissance, taken with Linescan shows aircraft on the ground. It also shows hot and cold engines and the signatures of departed aircraft.
Below: Trials installation of sensors for the Tornado reconnaissance system. The complete system is housed within the fuselage. The windows for the sideways-looking infra-red detectors are in the sides of the fuselage and the Linescan aperture is underneath the aircraft.

are today's successors to the wartime Storch, Auster and Grasshopper. Today's low-powered 'observation' aircraft, able in theory to operate from any convenient front-line field, include the Austrian HB-23 Scanliner, the British Optica Scout, the French Aéronautic 2000 and the US-German Egrett-1. The survivability of such machines is questionable, even though the French example, a true microlight, can carry anti-tank missiles. The most serious is the Egrett, resembling a long-span sailplane with a turboprop engine, giving it an operating height up to 59,000 ft (17,980 m). Both the Luftwaffe and USAF are showing interest in the military potential of this aircraft, which to a considerable degree has a stealth-type airframe. Not least of its desirable features is that it can loiter at 56,000 ft (17,070 m) for 12 hours.

Battlefield RPVs

Besides the new breed of stealth aircraft – which may be expected gradually to encompass all military aircraft, for whatever purpose – the only kind of aircraft that are difficult to detect are Remotely Piloted Vehicles (RPVs). These aircraft are small, so their signatures – RCS, visual, IR and noise – are small in proportion. In the years following 1945 the Ryan Company produced a series of target drones called Firebees. Gradually, these became a diverse family which included versions for attack and reconnaissance. Numerous shot-down examples of various models, notably the 147SK, were displayed by China and North Vietnam. In effect, they were miniature jet aircraft, and it is significant that hardly any aircraft in this class are in production today.

The emphasis appears, so far as the public is concerned, to have swung entirely towards even smaller RPVs for tactical battlefield use. Many of today's reconnaissance RPVs do not even go beyond the Line of Sight (LOS) from the operator. They are actually flown in real time by a human pilot, unlike drones, which are pilotless aircraft that fly according to prearranged commands stored inside their computer

memory. The only unusual factor is that the pilot is not on board. With bigger vehicles in the Firebee class, the pilot might be in a 'mother aircraft' such as a C-130, but today's battlefield RPVs invariably respond to commands from a pilot on the ground.

Battlefield RPVs include small piston-engined machines, some jets and even a strange form of helicopter which is one of a series of products from Canadair of Montreal. The first of this series was the CL-89, which after long development went into production with NATO designation USD-501. About 600 had been delivered by 1985 to the armies of the UK, West Germany, Italy and France.

Launched by a tandem boost rocket, the USD-501 looks like a missile, with four small wings around its 8 ft

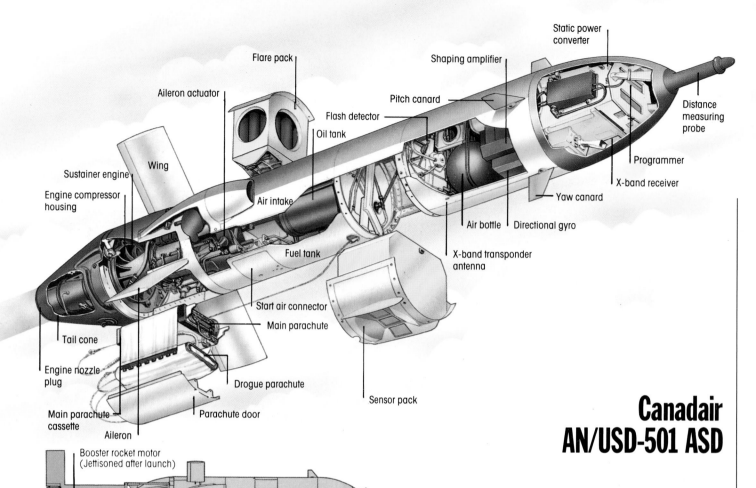

Static power converter

Shaping amplifier

Flare pack

Aileron actuator

Pitch canard

Flash detector

Oil tank

Distance measuring probe

Programmer

X-band receiver

Sustainer engine

Wing

Engine compressor housing

Air intake

Yaw canard

Air bottle

Directional gyro

X-band transponder antenna

Fuel tank

Start air connector

Main parachute

Tail cone

Engine nozzle plug

Drogue parachute

Main parachute cassette

Parachute door

Aileron

Sensor pack

Booster rocket motor (Jettisoned after launch)

Canadair
AN/USD-501 ASD

Above: The components of an AN/USD-501 surveillance drone. Left: The drone and booster rocket, which falls away as soon as the drone has accelerated.

6 in (2.62 m) body. A miniature turbojet drives it and its camera and IR linescan at about 460 mph (740 km/h) out to a distance of about 35 miles (56 km). Recovery is by parachute. This aircraft has now been developed into the CL-289 (USD-502) which is a joint product of Canadair and the German company Dornier. It is bigger, faster, longer-ranged and carries extra sensors, including a real-time video data link.

Canadair's third product is the CL-227 Sentinel. It looks like an upright peanut, less than 5 ft (1.5 m) tall and fitted with contra-rotating helicopter rotors, giving it VTOL capability. The Sentinel can be launched free, when it can fly out to a distance of about 31 miles (50 km), or it can be launched on a tether. Its surveillance horizon is extended to 30 miles on a 656-ft (200-m) cable and to 50 miles (80 km) on a 1,640-ft (500-m) cable. The Sentinel Phase 3 can carry daylight or low-level TV, a laser target designator, thermal (IR) imager, radiation (Elint) detector or decoy equipment.

Counting the Soviet Union as one, at least 66 companies around the world are working on reconnaissance or surveillance RPVs. There are also many amateur groups operating RPVs. In April 1989 details were published of a video-carrying helicopter RPV developed by a police team in Britain's Midlands to help in crime detection. Most of these RPVs are small, with a span from 6 ft to 20 ft (1.83-6.1 m) and a piston engine

of 2 hp to about 50 hp (1.5 to 37.5 kW). Several types have seen active service, notably the Mastiff and Scout developed in Israel.

Mastiff was developed by Tadiran Ltd in the mid-1970s. It entered service with the Israeli Army in 1979, and has been followed by the Mastiff 2 and 3. Mastiff 3 has a 22-hp (16.5-kW) two-stroke engine in a pusher installation at the rear of a box-like fuselage. The twin-finned tail is carried on slender booms. It weighs 170 lb (77 kg) when empty, takes 53 lb (24 kg) of fuel and can

Below: Mastiff 3, the remotely piloted reconnaissance vehicle developed by Tadiran Ltd and flown with outstanding successes by the Israeli Army.

Real-time monitoring

During the Battle of Fleurus in 1794 the French commander, Gen Jourdan, was able to receive signals in real time (without delay) from an observer in a balloon who could see the whole battle. In World War II, typical aerial reconnaissance was achieved after delays of from two to six hours while the aircraft went to and from its target and the films were developed, printed and interpreted. Real-time reconnaissance remained an apparently unattainable objective, but in recent years ground force commanders have come close to it.

Instant reconnaissance poses two problems: survivability of the air vehicle and survivability of the data link. Tiny RPVs not much bigger than radio-controlled model aircraft seem harmless, but modern soldiers know that the information they convey can be deadly. It would seem simplicity itself to shoot them down, yet during fighting over the Bekaa Valley in 1982 Israeli RPVs – engaged mainly in Elint (electronic reconnaissance), a particularly important form of information gathering – showed themselves to be highly survivable.

Their output – the exact details of several front-line electronic systems – enabled the Israeli Defence Forces to tune, adjust or program their own counter-measures for maximum effectiveness. Without such prior knowledge, supplied in real time, the most sophisticated ECM system is useless. The Israelis used the AGM-45 Shrike and AGM-88 HARM anti-radar missiles, but these could not home on their targets without being previously tuned to the target's wavelength and programmed with the target's waveform. It was precise real-time knowledge of the emissions of the SA-6 missile guidance radars that enabled IDF/AF attack aircraft to deploy countermeasures, enabling them to return from their missions.

Survivability of the air vehicle is probably enhanced by making recon RPVs smaller and faster. The Israeli RPVs had a wingspan of over 16 ft (4.9 m) and flew at just over 60 mph (96 km/h). In contrast, the CL-289 (NATO USD-502), the initial users of which are France, West Germany and Canada, has a span of 4 ft 4 inches (1.32 m) and flies at well over 500 mph (800 km/h). Despite modern SAMs and radar-laid flak, such RPVs are elusive targets. In such cases the only real problem is the second one: survivability of the data link.

Some of the first battlefield RPVs were guided back to their starting point. Then they either ejected an exposed roll of film or the imagery had to be recovered from the vehicle after it had landed. This method has the advantage of security; it cannot be interfered with by the enemy. The need for real-time results eliminates this method. Instead a radio data link is used. But the available payload is always severely limited, and a data link must have an electronic input.

For example, the CL-289 normally carries an SAT Corsaire IRLS (Infra-red linescan) and a Carl Zeiss KRb8/24D three-lens reconnaissance camera. The French SAT company linked the IRLS with a data link to output the thermal imagery back at the base station in real time. This is of value to a force commander, and the CL-289 has the range and target-coverage capability to be used at Corps level. The high-definition photographic images cannot be transmitted by the link. They have to be brought back and processed, and this degrades real time into perhaps half an hour.

If a commander has to have information instantly then there must be a radio link. Such a link can be interfered with by the enemy, most notably by jamming on the same frequency. One solution is to use spread-spectrum methods, such as Frequency Hopping (FH) in which the equipment switches rapidly and randomly between many frequencies.

A second solution is to convert the analog signal to digital pulses, which can be processed to defeat jamming. Both these solutions eat into the RPV's small payload. A third solution is to use a lower frequency which is reflected from the ionosphere; the RPV then has a strongly directional transmitting antenna which sends the beam almost straight up, the reflected beam then being aimed at the base station. This almost eliminates enemy jamming but there are other problems. In reality real-time monitoring is never obtained easily.

carry an equipment load of 81 lb (37 kg), giving a maximum take-off weight of 304 lb (138 kg).

Mastiff 3 can reach 115 mph (185 km/h) but normally cruises at 61 mph (98 km/h) for up to 7 h 30 min. The useful load can comprise a TV camera which can be aimed anywhere in the hemisphere beneath the RPV, or a pivoted TV camera plus a panoramic film camera, or a miniature FLIR and laser designator, or various electronic-warfare payloads. It can carry a warhead, or use reflective lenses to simulate much larger aircraft or even ships.

Tadiran's products spurred Israel Aircraft Industries to produce the Scout. This is similar to Mastiff 3 but slightly larger, weighing typically 350 lb (140 kg).

Mastiffs can make free take-offs, and lands normally, braked by an arrester wire. Scout is fired from a truck-mounted pneumatic catapult, and on landing is flown into a recovery net. Each Scout can carry a TV camera with telephoto/zoom lens, able to be aimed anywhere beneath, and a Perkin Elmer or equivalent panoramic camera scanning up to 60° each side of the flight path. These sensors can be replaced by a thermal imaging (IR) camera, laser designator or other equipment.

Large numbers of RPVs, mainly Scouts, have been used by the Israeli Army. They played a central role in the fighting over the Bekaa Valley in the spring and early summer of 1982, in the Israeli occupation of most of The Lebanon. For example, the Israeli Defence

RPV systems

In February 1985, GEC Avionics was selected by the British MoD(PE) as prime contractor for the British Army's RPV, the Phoenix. This is the first pilotless aircraft system to go into service with the British Army offering real-time remote targeting and battlefield surveillance. Major subcontractors include Flight Refuelling, which builds the air vehicle and is also responsible for the launch and recovery systems, Hunting Hivolt (Military Division), Scicon, and Marconi Command and Control Systems.

The British Army's primary requirement was for real-time surveillance of hostile areas by day, night or in poor visibility. it was specified that definition of targets should be good enough for positive recognition and further analysis. The Phoenix is expected to spend most of its time in support of long-range artillery. Having developed the system, the prime contractor points out that it can also be used for other missions, such as Electronic Warfare (EW), air-defence suppression, laser designation, Nuclear, Biological and Chemical (NBC) monitoring and as a communications relay platform or as a decoy vehicle.

For the air vehicle, the optimum configuration was found to be a tractor monoplane with a central nacelle and twin-boom tail. The 25-hp (18.75-kW) Normalair-Garrett WAEL 342 engine is mounted on a hinge at the front, driving a two-blade fixed-pitch propeller. On top is a crushable recovery module, with the recovery parachute housed in the tail of the nacelle. All parts are modular, made of a radar-absorbent plastics sandwich.

After prolonged study and research the best sensor was a single Thermal Imaging Common Module Class II (TICMII). This is mounted in a 360° turret giving a completely unobstructed view throughout the scene below the vehicle. The turret is mounted in a large underslung pod which is roll-stabilized, so the sensor can stay on target during banked turns, always with the horizon at the top of the viewed image. The associated optics give x2.5 to x10 magnification. The pod includes the associated cryogenic (refrigeration) system.

The final solution for the data link was an RF link

Force/Air Force claimed to have destroyed 19 Syrian SA-6 mobile SAM systems without loss. In 1973 similar missiles had decimated Israeli aircraft, which had no countermeasures against the SA-6's continuous-wave radar guidance. In 1982 constant surveillance of the SA-6 missiles by the Israeli RPVs revealed every detail of their guidance frequency, waveform and counter-countermeasure.

Even in such a seemingly perilous battle environment, hardly any of the RPVs were lost. In 1984 Tadiran and Israel Aircraft industries merged to form a special RPV company called Mazlat. This company has exported

using a highly directional flat-plate (radar type) gimballed antenna at both ends of the payload pod. Each antenna has perfect visibility within a complete hemisphere (front or rear, related to the vehicle) and switching from one to the other is automatic, depending on the orientation of the vehicle to the Ground Control Station (GCS). The link provides for command signals from ground to air and for video and 'housekeeping' signals from air to ground. The vehicle can follow completely preprogrammed tracks or it can be commanded throughout the mission by the Air Vehicle Controller (AVC). The usual mode combines both.

The GCS houses a crew of three. The Mission Controller receives and sorts tasks into missions, implements mission priorities, executes or replans missions and interfaces with tasking agencies (the whole system is designed to interface with BATES and other C^3 functions). The AVC generates and executes the flight plans, controls the air vehicle throughout the task and initiates autonomous flight modes.

The Image Analyst (IA) plans the search patterns, programmes the sensor scan mode, controls the scan by 'flying' the sensor ground footprint using a joystick, controls the zoom telescope image and detects, recognises, identifies and marks targets. Normally the mission controller faces a display of a large map of the area, the AVC faces a large digital map on which continuously appears the track of the vehicle and the footprint of the sensor, and the IA faces a display showing the sensor image in real time.

The Phoenix vehicle is carried on a self-contained launcher which is pallet-mounted and fits on a wide variety of army vehicles. The pallet includes a pump/generator power pack, hydraulic crane for reloads, de-icing and decontamination, air-vehicle engine start and warm-up, and an access platform. Launch is by pneumatic catapult; vehicles can be launched in quite rapid succession. Recovery is by parachute, deployed by data-link command from the rear of the fuselage. In descent the vehicle is inverted, landing on a crushable fairing. The impact does not damage the sensor pod, which is remote from the impact.

Left: The solar High-Altitude Powered Platform proposed by Lockheed is being considered by NASA for applications such as the monitoring of crops in California's Central Valley within this decade.
Right: An inflatable dinghy underway after being deployed from an airship. Missions of surveillance, targeting, airborne early warning and communications are being considered for similar specially designed airships which are inexpensive to buy and run.

numerous RPVs, mainly of the upgraded Scout 800 type, many of which have seen active service with South African forces in Namibia.

Aerial platforms

Aerial surveillance aircraft are often called platforms. Some are especially well qualified for such a title. One is the High-Altitude Powered Platform (HAPP), yet another Lockheed development. Most of the funding for HAPP has been for civilian uses, but it has military potential, because it could in theory lift a reconnaissance sensor 65,000-70,000 ft (19,800-21,300 m) and keep it there continuously. Missions of about a year are envisaged.

HAPP would look like a giant sailplane, with a span of perhaps 322 ft (98 m). A small pusher propeller would be driven by a 15-hp (11-kW) electric motor supplied with current by solar cells covering the wings by day and by solar-charged fuel cells at night. It would take about 4 hours to spiral up to station, thereafter cruising at about 60 mph (97 km/h), which is significantly greater than winds at such altitudes.

The other aircraft which can truly be called a platform is the airship. The proposed Sentinel 5000 (US Navy designation YEZ-2A) would be 425 ft (130 m) long and have a non-rigid gas envelope, a gross volume of just over 2.5 million cu ft (21,580 cu m) and a normal operating height of 5,000-10,000 ft (1,520-3,050 m).

Chapter 2

STRATEGY AND TACTICS:

The Pacific Basin

The western rim of the Pacific Region is in a fascinating state of flux. Not only are Japan and China on the verge of becoming genuine world powers, with China at least possessing the ability and desire to project its influence beyond its own frontiers, but a number of the lesser regional powers are also longing to be in charge of their own future.

The influence of the USA and, to a lesser extent, the USSR is still strong and neither show a desire to change. Added to this fact, the instability of many regimes in the region and the unresolved frontier disputes make some form of conflict appear inevitable.

A Thai and a US soldier taking part in Cobra Gold – one of the frequent joint exercises undertaken by the US in the Pacific. US current command structure is based in Hawaii where the Commander in Chief Pacific (CINCPAC) – normally an Admiral – has his headquarters.

Three of the world's four most populous countries (China, the USSR and the USA) and three of the world's largest economies (the USA, the USSR and Japan) form part of the Pacific Basin. Because of the great distances involved (even today, it takes 11 hours to fly by subsonic jet from Los Angeles to Tokyo), some parts of the Basin are, in practice, isolated from the rest of the Pacific. This applies particularly to the eastern seaboard, where only the USA and, to a much lesser extent, Canada have the power to project their military and political influence across the ocean.

For several centuries the Atlantic, and particularly Western Europe, has been the centre of world affairs, but changes are apparent. The 'economic miracle' of Japan, the re-emergence of China as a great power, the massive growth in the economies of states such as South Korea, Taiwan and Singapore, and the shift to the western coast in the USA (and Canada) are all part of a change that has come about since 1945.

Some observers believe that this process is irreversible, and that states on the western seaboard of the Pacific are the ones that will matter in the next century. This view is stretching current developments too far. South Korea and Taiwan are experiencing the problems of advanced economies; in other regions countries such

Above: Aftermath of the atomic bomb. The Shimomuna Watch shop in Hiroshima in 1946, a year after a US plane dropped a single atom bomb over the centre of the city.

as India and Brazil – despite current problems – are showing signs of becoming dominant; and, not least, the Atlantic powers are self-sufficient in ways that not even Japan has yet achieved.

There has, however, been a fundamental change. NATO powers – the USA in particular – and the European orientation of the USSR are still extremely important, but one part of the world does not and cannot dominate the rest to the extent it used to.

Reorganization

Until the Japanese bid for regional dominance began in 1932, much of the western Pacific seaboard and most of the islands were colonies or dependencies of European powers, and the USA – then as now – held many other Pacific islands 'in trust'. China, wracked by internal feuding, was not a major factor in the region, and the USSR appeared more than contained by the Japanese armed forces. The only other independent state was Thailand, then of negligible significance.

The ease with which the Japanese pushed back the Western powers came as a revelation to the various groups seeking independence. It encouraged them to form sovereign states when Japan was pushed back in its turn. Decolonization is still not complete – France and the USA (with its 'trust territories' held under UN mandates) being the worst offenders – but most of the original colonial powers have now withdrawn.

Left: A jungle grave for a French soldier. France is the only major European nation to retain extensive colonial interests in the Pacific region.

The reorganization itself, however, led to a number of wars, confrontations, and internal conflicts within states. In addition, it left a legacy of political and military problems for the defeated power, Japan. Although the post-war occupation was technically on behalf of all the Allied powers, the Americans under General Douglas MacArthur did not allow other powers any say.

His administration imposed a constitution on Japan in November 1945. Article 9 renounced war and the threat of force as a means of settling international disputes. It also said that land, sea and air forces, as well as 'other war potential' would never be maintained. When the Americans encouraged Japan to re-arm in the aftermath of the Korean War, this stipulation became a problem. The Defence Agency Establishment Law and Self-Defence Forces Law, adopted in July 1954, got around this problem by setting up the army, navy and air force as Japanese Self-Defence Forces (JSDFs) and forbidding troops from being sent out of the country. These forces were designated the JGSDF (G for Ground), JMSDF (M for Maritime) and JASDF (A for Air) respectively.

During this period of reorganization, the USA – which had begun by encouraging European powers to leave the area – constructed a network of mainly short-lived alliances involving remaining European powers and local administrations to oppose what it saw as an all-embracing communist menace. SEATO and ANZUS covered South East Asia and the South Pacific, and there were bilateral treaties with most friendly states.

Below: Chinese nationalist soldiers load ammunition aboard LST 772 as evacuation operations continue during the civil war between nationalists and communists. Evacuees were taken to Keelung, Formosa.

The wars

Since 1945, there have been several wars which have taken place on the western rim of the Pacific. The main problem has been artificial borders and the aftermath of decolonization (as with the two Koreas and Vietnams), sometimes complicated by ideology.

The Korean War resulted from the aftermath of the 40-year Japanese occupation of the country. With the USSR occupying the North and the USA organizing a regime in the South, it was not possible to re-unite the state. The North, under President Kim Il Sung, decided on a pre-emptive strike to re-unify the country. President Rhee of South Korea was not popular, and the South's armed forces were limited.

The initial invasion on June 25 1950 was extremely successful, and despite the agreement of the UN (due to a temporary Soviet boycott) to support the South, the North reduced the UN troops (nearly all Americans) to a small perimeter around the port of Pusan in southeast Korea. A brilliant but risky amphibious counterstroke by General MacArthur at Inchon forced the North Koreans to fall back beyond their own borders. But MacArthur overreached himself by ordering a pursuit up to the Chinese border.

The Chinese responded with massive infantry attacks, driving the UN forces back in confusion. MacArthur wanted to use nuclear weapons, and partly because of this he was dismissed by President Truman. The front stabilized near the original frontier of the 38th parallel and, after two more years of fighting, the cease-fire – first discussed in 1951 – was signed on July 27 1953. Talks continue at Panmunjon to this day to try to resolve outstanding issues.

The Vietnam War was undoubtedly the longest since 1945. The communist regime, after being excluded

from the South, first drove out the French from the North by mid-1954. Guerrilla warfare started in 1946, and after the communist Vietminh failed in conventional offensives in 1951, the French made the mistake of making a stand at an isolated up-country village called Dien Bien Phu. Despite US assistance, this post was first isolated in late 1953 then overrun in May 1954 – a psychological shock that resulted in the partition of the two Vietnams at the Geneva Conference later that same year.

The Americans, thinking Vietnam the key to all of southeast Asia, gradually increased their support to South Vietnam, although the repressive nature of the regimes they supported, from Diem onwards, made it difficult to unite South Vietnam against the communist insurgency promoted by the North. After the Gulf of Tonkin incident in August 1964, US aid was increased, and the USA formally joined the war in mid-1965. With considerable help from South Korea and Australia, US regular forces (eventually numbering more than 525,000 troops) tried to eliminate the Viet Cong guerrillas.

The Tet Offensive of 1968 – although a military disaster for the North – was a political victory. It gave the impression that the war was unwinnable by the South, and resulted in the Paris peace talks of May 1968. The Nixon administration was mainly concerned with extracting the USA from the war, and used US military muscle, particularly bombing northern cities and mining their ports, to extricate regular US troops by August 1972. Without US support, the South Vietnamese lasted longer than many expected, but were overwhelmed by the final communist push in April 1975.

After the fall of South Vietnam, the Lon Nol military regime that had overthrown Prince Sihanouk in Cambodia (Kampuchea) was itself overthrown – after US procrastination – by the communist Khmer Rouge regime of Pol Pot in April 1975. Pol Pot proceeded with a large-scale campaign of extermination, but his regime was itself ousted by a Vietnamese invasion by 12 divisions in December 1978. The Khmer Rouge returned to guerrilla warfare, and the Vietnamese were themselves the target of an invasion this time by 33 Chinese divisions on March 17 1979.

The Chinese captured the major town of Lang Son, but suffered severe casualties despite Vietnamese inadequacies. They soon withdrew and, despite a second flare-up of fighting, left Vietnam in possession of most of Kampuchea. The Khmer Rouge, however, continued guerrilla warfare along the Thai border, and by the end of 1988 the Vietnamese had withdrawn, leaving a shaky puppet regime and a chaotic situation throughout Kampuchea – once more (in 1989) renamed Cambodia.

Left: The Soviet Union and the USA are separated in the Arctic (near Alaska) by only a narrow strait. They share the Pacific Basin with Japan and China and other nations aspiring to attain super-power status.

Confrontations

Confrontations – a word used to mean anything from the possibility of fighting to open hostilities that neither of the combatants wish to describe as war – is a convenient way of summarizing many of the actions that have taken place in the Pacific Basin since 1945. Although some of these involved China, Japan, Taiwan, South Korea and Indo-China, most of them concerned Indonesia.

Indonesia, unlike most other states in the region, had to fight for its independence. The Japanese set up an Indonesian regime after they conquered the Netherlands East Indies in 1942. This regime later fought the Japanese, but inherited much Japanese military equipment when the Japanese surrendered. When the Dutch returned (with British aid), they had to fight to regain control, and on December 27 1949 they gave up the struggle and agreed to the independence of Indonesia – originally proclaimed on August 17 1945.

Plagued by internal dissension, Indonesia pursued an aggressive foreign policy – so much so that the US Navy had to send a destroyer division through the Lombok and Mahassi Straits in January 1958 to counter Indonesian claims to be able to close them to navigation. Indonesia was bolstered by large shipments of arms from the USSR between 1959 and 1964, although it used little of them in combat, but its troops saw action in both the east and west of the islands.

To the east, Netherlands New Guinea (now West Irian) was the scene of clashes with the Dutch, including one on January 1962 that resulted in the sinking of the Indonesian Motor Torpedo Boat *Madjan Tutul*. This confrontation ended when the Dutch handed the territory over to the UN later in 1962 (the UN promptly giving trusteeship to Indonesia, which annexed it after a farcical 'plebiscite' in 1969).

Above: A Private of H Company, 2nd Battalion, Fifth Marine Regiment receives treatment for wounds sustained during Operation Hue City in Vietnam in 1968.

To the west, 1962 also saw the start of the four-year confrontation over parts of Borneo. This was the period of the formation of the federation of Malaysia (1963), and Indonesia tried to claim the whole island of Borneo for itself. British armed forces were heavily committed, and the situation was resolved (in 1966) only after the Indonesian Army removed President Sukharno and crushed the Indonesian communists. The Five Power Defence Agreement of 1971 still safeguards Malaysia and Singapore against a repeat performance.

More recently, the Indonesian armed forces took part in the largest opposed amphibious operation for a decade when they seized East Timor. This used to be a Portuguese colony but, after internal unrest, the Portuguese abdicated power to Fretilin in September 1975. The successful invasion took place three months later, making East Timor Indonesia's 27th province.

In China at the end of World War II, nationalists and communists resumed their interrupted civil war. US troops and warships were involved in a number of incidents, including landing 1,500 US Marines at Tsingtao in November 1948. The British were caught up in the Civil War too – most notably in the Yangtse Incident when the frigate *Amethyst* was trapped on the Yangtse from April to July 1949.

After the nationalists conceded defeat and withdrew to the offshore islands in December 1949, the US 7th Fleet became the guarantor of their continued existence. It could not prevent the Chinese Army overrunning Hainan Island in 1950, but on several occasions in the 1950s – most notably in June 1950, February 1955 and September 1958 – it interposed US ships between the

two sides. The 7th Fleet not only enabled the nationalists to set up a new state on Taiwan, they also allowed it to keep a foothold on Quemoy and Matsu Islands, within close artillery range of the Chinese mainland.

Japanese post-war weakness, and the seizing of Sakhalin Island and the Kuriles by the USSR in 1945, have resulted in a series of incidents from 1945 onwards. Most have involved fishing boats rather than armed forces, but by 1969 Japanese fishermen found themselves virtually excluded from the Sea of Okhotsk, and from waters claimed by China and South Korea. South Korean armed forces seized Takeshima Island in 1954 – a dispute that is still unresolved.

Following the cease-fire in 1953, there have been actions between ships of North and South Korea as both sides tried to infiltrate spies into the other's territory. These were most intense in 1969 and 1974. There have also been disturbances along the cease-fire line, as well as the discovery in November 1974 of three tunnels – the largest 6 x 6 ft (1.8 x 1.8 m) in cross section and 2.7 miles (4.4 km) long – leading from the North to behind South Korean lines.

After the Geneva conference of 1954 gave full independence to the countries making up French Indo-China, there have been continual frontier squabbles, as well as the various Vietnam wars. In addition to incidents involving Vietnam, Laos, Cambodia (Kampuchea) and China, in various combinations, Thai armed forces have lost aircraft and men over the years in actions against the various regimes in Cambodia.

Left: A tunnel dug by North Koreans into the South. The South Korean Authorities claimed it was to be used to place North Korean Army units behind the 38th Parallel.

Internal conflicts

It is not surprising that decolonization has resulted in a large number of internal conflicts, as various factions struggle for power. There have been waves of rebellion since 1945, mostly either due to communist guerrillas or military unrest. In rare instances, such as the secession of Singapore from Malaysia in August 1965, following Chinese-Malay clashes, conflict has been avoided. Many countries, however, have been plagued by unrest.

One of the first communist uprisings was in Malaya, following the British resumption of power after World War II. The 'emergency' lasted from 1948 to 1960, and the communist leader and some of his supporters still hold out in the area around the Thai border to this day. The uprising was defeated by firm action by the British Army, including removing rural villagers to 'defended villages' to deny food and information to the communists. The regular forces were helped considerably by racial tension between the mainly Chinese communists and the majority Malay population. After World War II stocks were used up, interrupted supplies caused insuperable difficulties for the insurgents.

Indonesia has always had internal problems, as well as the external confrontations. By far the most serious was the nationalist South Moluccan rebellion of the early 1950s, which had Dutch support. The communist PKI Party, which had considerable influence in the 1950s and early 1960s, attempted a coup in October 1965 but were massacred by the army which installed General Suharto as President.

Besides the struggle in Vietnam, there was continual conflict in Laos between the communist Pathet Lao and

Below: Chinese citizens during the Cultural Revolution inspired by Mao Zedong (depicted in poster) scan newspapers – the primary source of news then.

the Royal Laotian Army from 1953. For a time, the country was partitioned, but as the North finally succeeded in Vietnam, the Pathet Lao took over Laos – only for it to be overrun soon afterwards by the Vietnamese Army.

Much the same happened in Cambodia. Prince Sihanouk weaved a skillful neutralist path for many years, but as the Vietnamese War intensified the communist Khmer Rouge became more powerful. A US-inspired army coup ousted Sihanouk, only for the Khmer Rouge to take over and slaughter their opponents. They in turn were pushed back into guerrilla warfare by the Vietnamese Army.

In the Philippines, the communist Huk guerrillas first fought the Japanese from 1942, then – eventually reorganized as the PKP – they fought the government until the army reduced their effectiveness in the early 1950s. Despite the revival of the Communist New People's Army by Jose Sison in 1968 and the outbreak of the Moro rebellion in the early 1970s, it was the conventional opposition led by Cory Aquino that finally overthrew the Marcos regime in February 1986.

In the 1950s and 1960s, American strategists were convinced that if one country in Indo-China fell under communist control, the rest would inevitably follow. Known as the Domino Theory, this ignored the strongly nationalist tilt of all the parties involved, and although what was French Indo-China is now under various forms of communist rule, the communists were contained in Malaysia, Indonesia and the Philippines, and the important opposition to the right-wing military dictatorships in Thailand and Burma has always been nationalist or tribal, rather than communist.

In China, although the effects of the Cultural Revolution that began in January 1966 were as devastating as any rebellion, it is unique in that it was inspired by the government itself. Stemming from the tensions caused by the formation of the Chinese state and armed forces in 1949, this 'revolution' enabled Chairman Mao Zedong (Tse Tung) and his supporters to retain power until he died almost a decade later; but it left the country, its industry and armed forces in tatters.

The Basin today

There are enormous variations of size, wealth, population, political and military circumstances and aspirations of the countries making up the Basin. The similarities and differences between Singapore and Indonesia exemplify most countries in the region. Singapore is a small cluster of islands – the largest of which (Singapore Island) is no bigger than Rhode Island or the Isle of Wight. It has negligible mineral wealth and exists from trade and commerce. With a population of only 2.7 million, and a Gross Domestic Product (GDP) of about $US 18.6 billion, the average income is about $US 6,700 per head. The defence budget for the 55,000-strong armed forces is just over $US 1 billion.

Indonesia is vastly different. An archipelago of

Above: A British soldier with a Corporal of the Gurkha Military Police on patrol in Malaya. After 12 years of 'emergency', communist uprisings were defeated and independence gained in 1957.

several thousand islands, stretching over 3,200 miles (5,100 km) from east to west, it exploits its considerable oil deposits and other mineral wealth to produce a GDP of about $US 90 billion but, with a population of more than 184 million, the average income is only about $US 340 per head. The defence budget is only about $US 1.5 billion, with nearly 300,000 in the armed forces.

There are, however, some common points. They meet geographically at the Straits of Singapore and are members of ASEAN.

China is modernizing its armed forces and is approaching the stage where it can project its power over long distances. It cannot yet be considered a superpower, because it lacks the sophisticated technology and infrastructure to compare with the USA and USSR, but the scale of its armed forces and the speed of its modernization make it only a matter of time.

China is the only purely Pacific power that possesses nuclear weapons and the means to deliver them. It exploded its first atomic bomb in October 1964 and its first hydrogen bomb in June 1967. It is now replacing its shorter range missiles with the Dong Feng (East Wind) ICBMs, although its bomber force – they are still building the H-6 (a version of the 1950s Soviet Tu-16 Badger) – leaves much to be desired.

It has three nuclear submarines in service and three more under construction. These are Xia SSBNs (nuclear ballistic missile submarines) and Han SSNs (nuclear-powered attack submarines). Despite major setbacks in development, and with considerable Western assistance, the first submerged firing of the Chinese naval ICBM took place in 1982 from the Soviet-supplied Golf diesel submarine, and the first from a Han took place in September 1989.

The rest of the navy is gradually being re-equipped, and is at last capable of overseas deployments. The sheer scale of the army (it is being reduced from over 3 million to about 2.5 million) makes re-equipment difficult, and it badly needs better main battle tanks and motorized artillery. However, the army is being reorganized to improve its overall effectiveness. The air force is acquiring improved aircraft, such as the F-8 Finback and Q-5 Fantan, although these are years behind Soviet and US developments. Warning systems are also being updated, with OTH-B (Over The Horizon-Backscatter) radar to give long-range detection.

Japan has just surpassed the 1 per cent GNP level on defence funding – a limitation it adopted itself in the late 1960s, although it is restricting itself to 'defensive' weapons and force structures. Japan's neighbours are extremely wary of its intentions, and attempts to revise views on Japan's wartime role – such as Prime Minister Nakasone's bellicose statements in the early 1980s, and government-inspired moves to rewrite school textbooks on World War II – meet strenuous opposition both inside and outside Japan.

The armed forces in Japan are by no means universally popular, as was shown by the reaction to the accidental sinking of a fishing boat by the JMSDF submarine *Nadashio* on surfacing in Tokyo Bay on July 23 1988, which ultimately resulted in the resignation of the Japanese Defence Agency director Tsutomo Karawa. However, Japan has the military and economic muscle to take a much stronger line, and it is likely that it may soon find the political will – and opportunity – to do so.

The current defence budget of more than $US 24 billion is enormous by most standards, and allows for the expansion envisaged by the then Prime Minister Nakasone when he agreed with President Reagan in May 1981 to increase the role of Japan's armed forces to defending the sea lanes out to 1,000 miles (1,600 km). This has been the basis for the Aegis destroyer and FSX fighter programme, as well as the enlarging of the P-3 Orion and E-2 Hawkeye force. It also covers the improved radar and control system installed after

the undetected and embarrassing arrival of a lost Soviet Mig-25 Foxbat.

Other expanding powers in the region include both the Koreas, although the South is outpacing the North economically. Taiwan, like the Koreas, has moved out of the low-cost manufacturing category into the developed world, and is in a position to provide all but the most sophisticated weapons to its armed forces.

There are also a group of states in the south-west that are doing relatively well and can afford to equip their armed forces with advanced equipment. These are Malaysia, Singapore and Brunei. In its defence policy, Brunei has more in common with the Gulf oil states than with its neighbours – it pays for a battalion of Gurkhas to provide the basis of its infantry, and can buy more weapons than it has trained troops to man them.

Bare existence

Some countries have not benefited from the post-war economic boom. Most of French Indo-China, including Vietnam, the Philippines and Burma, has seen little real development, and many nations there have poor incomes and large populations. Most maintain large armed forces – usually, large numbers of ill-equipped men with small

quantities of sophisticated equipment that is difficult to maintain.

The only exceptions are many of the Pacific Islands. They are also poor, but the distances between them and the neighbouring groups is such that they do not need large numbers of men under arms. Most are members of the Commonwealth.

Besides China (and, in times of tension, the USSR), the country with the largest number of troops under arms in the area is Vietnam. On an average yearly income per person of about $US 200, it has accepted that it cannot keep more than 1 million men under arms, so it is reorganizing its army into a much smaller regular force plus a citizen's militia. It has withdrawn most of its troops from Cambodia and has held talks with Thailand about reducing tension in the area. One economy has always been the tiny navy. In its place, the Soviet Pacific Fleet has been encouraged to use the old US facilities at Cam Ran Bay and Da Nang.

Some poor countries are better off, relatively, than others. For example, the Philippines have had to discard their F-8 Crusader fighters because they cannot afford the spares, whereas Indonesia has purchased new General Dynamics F-16s. Indonesia has just rebuilt its navy, but although many of the smaller vessels are new, the larger frigates are second-hand from the USA, Britain and The Netherlands.

In most of these countries, the military are either in power, or at least extremely influential, so they have done better than other groups within the state. However, even a slightly less-poor state like Thailand cannot buy the quantities of advanced equipment it needs. The loss in air display accidents of three out of

Above: Yushio-class patrol submarine of the Japanese Maritime Self-Defence Force.
Right: Japanese Air Self-Defence Force F-15J, licence-built by Mitsubishi. Article 9 of the Allied powers' constitution imposed on Japan after World War II disallowed Japan from maintaining land, sea and air forces. Following the Korean War, when the USA encouraged Japan to re-arm, the stipulation was changed in July 1954 by the Defence Agency Establishment Law and Self-Defences Forces Law. This designated Japanese Forces as Japanese Self-Defence Forces (JSDFs).

30 F-5E fighters was an economic catastrophe. This is why the Thai armed forces are buying limited quantities of Western equipment and larger numbers of the cheaper but less capable Chinese equivalents – such as the Type 69 tank.

The old powers

The scale of US military involvement in the Far East may be shrinking – at one stage it had defence treaties with eight countries in the area as well as Britain and France – but it is still immense. With the advent of the long-range Trident SLBM (Submarine-Launched Ballistic Missile) the Polaris Submarine base at Guam became redundant, but the facilities at Clark Air Force base and Subic Bay naval base in the Philippines are enormous. Their lease (the current one expires in 1991) underpins the shaky Philippines economy – it was worth $US 900 million between 1984 and 1988.

Since the Spanish-American War at the turn of the century, the USA has had a forwards policy in the Pacific. Their current command structure is based on Hawaii where the Commander in Chief Pacific (CINCPAC) – normally an Admiral – has his headquarters. His main

forces are the two US fleets, the 7th in the western Pacific, and the 3rd – for training and reinforcements – in the east. One carrier, *Midway*, has been home-ported at Yokosuka in Japan since the 1970s. There are major land forces in South Korea, and the air force has main bases there, and in Okinawa and the Philippines.

There are frequent exercises – both alone and with allies. The annual RIMPAC series, which started in 1971, involves warships and aircraft from the USA, Canada, Australia and (since 1982) Japan, with occasional British and (until 1986) New Zealand participation. Other joint exercises include Cobra Gold with Thailand, and a whole series with South Korea.

Sometimes political limitations prevent US forces from being used to best effect, as in the Vietnam War. Another example was the Pueblo incident. In 1975, force was used against Kampuchea (Cambodia) over the Mayuguez incident, whereas a three-carrier taskforce

Below: Team Spirit 87 – a US and Republic of Korean annual exercise to improve interoperability and team-work. A US Security Specialist shows his South Korean counterpart an M-203 Grenade Launcher.

Above: Chinese soldiers on parade. China's modernization and bid to super-power status are now expected to be slowed by the massacre in 1989 of students in Tiananmen Square. Above right: Civilians are not directly involved with the annual US-Korean Team Spirit exercises, but they identify with the operations and give assistance where they can.

could not take action after North Korean patrol boats seized the US intelligence ship *Pueblo* just inside international waters on January 23 1968. The crew had to endure 11 months of captivity until the USA 'apologised'.

By seizing the Kuriles and the southern half of Sakhalin Island from Japan in 1945, the USSR improved its strategic position in the Far East, but most of the exits for its Fleet to the open ocean are still controlled by Japan. The major exception is the main submarine base at Petropavlovsk, isolated on the tip of the Kamchatka peninsula.

The submarine fleet is the largest in the Soviet Navy, and the surface fleet is more powerful than any other in the region, except the USN. Despite an easing of the tension, powerful land forces are required to cover the long border with China, and for the same reason there is a formidable force of ICBMs and IRBMs in the Soviet Far Eastern Theatre.

The British decision to withdraw from east of Suez by 1971 took place as planned, leaving only the Singapore dockyard (handed over to Singapore in 1976) and Hong Kong – now mainly used by the USN and due to be returned to China in July 1997. Except for occasional exercises in the Pacific and isolated dots on the map, such as Pitcairn Island, little remains of the once

extensive British domination of large parts of the area. One final responsibility is the five-power treaty with Australia and New Zealand that provides commitments to the independence of Malaysia and Singapore.

By contrast, France has clung to its Pacific islands, with the exception of the New Hebrides, which were jointly owned with Britain. This is partly because of the use of Mururoa (and now once again Fangatufa) Island as a nuclear test site – involving in the late 1960s up to 40 per cent of the French surface navy – but also because it considers possessions such as New Caledonia to be a part of Metropolitan France, whatever the legal niceties. France currently has bases in French Polynesia (at Tahiti) and at Noumea and New Caledonia.

Australia and New Zealand had a defence review in 1986. The New Zealand review mainly concerned financial cuts, but the Dibbs Report completed a radical alteration in direction for the Australian armed forces. Rather than buy a carrier – but for the Falklands war this would have been the British *Invincible* – Australia is now building a three-tiered defence out to 1,000 miles from its shores. There will be OTH radar backed by AEW aircraft for early warning, and tanker aircraft to extend the range of the primary defence – the Australian Air Force F-18s and F-111s. New Swedish submarines are on order, and for the first time a major segment of the fleet will be based on the west coast.

Australia's major defence problems are the difficulty of retaining aircrew, despite large loyalty payments (they are poached by the airlines) and the expulsion of New Zealand from ANZUS. Australia and New Zealand, however, are collaborating on a frigate design to replace both countries' major surface warships. Australia retains close ties with the USA, and with the Pacific islands.

The Pacific Patrol Boat programme has provided practical assistance, and the Royal Australian Navy flies regular P-3C Orion patrol flights from the islands.

The arms industries

Throughout east and southeast Asia, arms industries are being developed from scratch – often with impressive results. Australia has a developed arms industry – not as large and capable as Japan's, but well suited to its needs. Other economies, such as North and South Korea, Singapore and Taiwan, have developed semi-sophisticated arms industries supporting well-equipped forces. Some countries, such as China and Indonesia, are large enough and have sufficient natural resources to develop an arms industry, despite their economic failings. Even the poorer countries, for example, Thailand and the Philippines, are trying to reduce their dependence on major arms suppliers.

Nevertheless, they remain arms importers. No country on the western edge of the Pacific rim, except the Soviet Union, is self-sufficient in weapons design and production. This dependence on imported arms has unwelcomed consequences – such as US insistence (until Vietnam acquired MiG-23 Flogger aircraft) that countries such as South Korea, Singapore, and Thailand bought the inferior F-16/79 or F-20 Tigershark rather than the F-16A, or Taiwan's difficulties since China and the USA resumed diplomatic relations – but they are serious enough to outweigh the massive expense of starting individual, national arms industries.

China was the first post-1945 state to found an industry. Although the USSR provided advanced weapons from the early 1950s, culminating in the October 1957 agreement which resulted in such transfers as the Golf class missile submarine, President Krushchev rescinded this agreement in June 1959 and China had to reverse-engineer (dismantle equipment, work out how to build it, then design manufacturing tools for producing the equipment) its Soviet-supplied equipment. The delays this caused were compounded by China's internal problems, and it was only in the 1980s – with considerable Western assistance – that most Chinese military hardware began to move out of the 1950s.

Chinese achievements are undoubtedly impressive. The early 1960s saw the development of atomic and hydrogen bombs and, eventually, the ICBMs to deliver them. More recently, there are the nuclear-powered Han-class attack and Xia-class SSBM submarines, C-801 cruise missiles and A-5 Fantan attack aircraft amongst many other examples of fairly sophisticated design. Such equipment has enabled China to become a major arms exporter. Until recently, most weapons exports went to North Korea; now they arm Iran, Egypt and Pakistan, as well as more than 30 other countries. The most significant single recent export – in the teeth of US opposition – was the sale of 90 CSS-2 IRBMs to Saudi Arabia.

Taiwan appears to be much more self-sufficient than it actually is, because (like China) it gives its own designation to items it licence-builds. For example, the Hsiung Feng missile is actually the Israeli Gabriel, although in Mark 2 form it has a Taiwanese-developed infra-red seeker head. Despite its immense arms expenditure, Taiwan cannot match China's production, so much of its energies go – as with the Hsiung Feng – into improving existing equipment.

The most important current project is the IDF (InDigenous Fighter) produced by AIDC (Aero Industry Development Centre). Because the USA refused to allow Taiwan to buy the F-20 Tigershark in 1982, it has developed its own twin-engined fighter. This, like the Japanese FSX, is a modification of the General Dynamics F-16, but whereas the Japanese fighter – with direct US support, despite disagreements, plus the Japanese economy and world-leading electronics industry behind it – is 'state-of-the-art', the Taiwanese variant is the best that can be done (with General Dynamics' assistance) in the circumstances. With two Garrett turbojets, its performance will be generally inferior to that of the original F-16, although better than most aircraft in Chinese service.

North and South Korea, spurred on by each other, have developed industries capable of building tanks and frigates and some types of aircraft, but South Korea – with twice the population – definitely has the edge. Both are arms exporters – North Korea notably to Iran – but only South Korea produces sophisticated equipment likely to appeal in an open market.

Indonesia started its own arms industry early, and

Left: Fast Patrol Boats are an economical option for navies with severely limited defence budgets, but they are beyond the reach of some of the poorest nations in the Pacific region. Below: The General Dynamics F-16 is the basis of the Japanese FSX fighter and the Taiwanese IDF fighter, which has limited capability.

the aircraft manufacturer ITPN is co-designer (with CASA of Spain) of the CN-235 transport, as well as licence-builder of aircraft and helicopters. However, Indonesia mainly builds other people's designs, such as Lurssen Fast Patrol Boats (FPBs) and Boeing hydrofoils. Likewise, Singapore (mainly the government-owned Singapore Technologies group of companies) builds FPBs and upgrades equipment such as A-4 Skyhawks. New Zealand has also been upgrading its

Above: Chinese Helix telemetry antenna. Chinese technology in navigation and weapons control is developing rapidly to match its nuclear status.

A-4s, and has much the same capabilities.

The poorer countries that make some of their own equipment operate at a very low level. For example, the Philippines licence-build Pilatus BN Islander twin-prop utility aircraft. Otherwise, the most that is manufactured is small arms and ammunition.

Japanese arms
In the immediate aftermath of World War II, the Japanese arms industry was totally converted to civilian products. With the emergence of the Self Defence Force in the 1950s, however, a limited capacity to produce weapons was revived. Most of the well-known names, such as Mitsubishi and Kawasaki, survived but all the major weapons systems were either American, such as the JASDF's F-86 Sabre fighters, or closely based on US technology, like the JGSDF's Type 61 main battle tank (basically a reduced M-48 that took advantage of the smaller Japanese soldier). Gradually, Japanese content increased, but the close relationship with US designs has continued.

For political reasons post-war Japan has never devoted the resources to military research and development that would enable it to be as self-sufficient in arms design as, for example, Britain or France, or even West Germany. So the Aegis destroyers will be slightly modified versions of the USN's Arleigh Burke class, whereas previous major JMSDF warships used US equipment and weapons in Japanese hulls. Despite a defence budget that exceeds 1 per cent of the GNP for the first time since the early 1960s, there is insufficient money to develop new naval hulls and systems as well as the FSX and other advanced equipment.

The Aegis's hulls, machinery and systems will actually be built in Japan and there will be some transfer of technology. Despite American desire to reduce their $50 billion trading deficit with Japan, US industry sees Japan, correctly, as their most threatening commercial competitor and wishes to protect those areas where the USA has a technological lead over Japan. These conflicting pressures have resulted in problems over the FSX sea-lane defence fighter.

To the disappointment of the Japanese aircraft industry, the chosen SX-3 design was a modified US General Dynamics F-16, rather than a totally Japanese design, in deference to the trade imbalance. Despite formal agreements on technology transfer between Japan and the USA (the first was signed in September 1986) the major difficulties concern the electronics. In the preceding F-15J fighters, details of crucial parts of the software were retained by the USA. With the SX-3, Japan wanted to modify these computer codes themselves. In return, the USA demanded access to design details of the Japanese advanced active phased-array radar modules. As Japan slowly becomes less reliant on the USA, such disputes can only become more common.

The size of the Defence Force and the sophistication

of its weapons is such that despite the prohibition on exporting weapons, Japan is becoming a force to be reckoned with in weapons production. Examples are missiles for all three services – the Misubishi Type 80 anti-ship missile for the JASDF and (later) for the JMSDF and the Toshiba Type 81 truck-mounted surface-to-air missile for the JGSDF. Unless costs can be spread by selling equipment abroad, however, Japan is going to continue to be dependent on foreign (mainly US) research and development for many years.

Unrest

Although some long-standing problems have been removed, there are many unresolved disputes, both between and inside states, to which badly drawn frontiers, racial tensions and ideology all contribute. The Philippines has two internal problems; first the supporters of Ferdinand Marcos have never really accepted the Aquino regime, and, second, the large-scale communist insurgency in the central islands shows no sign of being contained. Thailand and Burma have problems with frontier infringements and dissident hill tribes, and in Burma especially there is ever-increasing public disquiet about the ruling military junta.

In what used to be French Indo-China, only Vietnam appears stable; after the exodus of the boat people the South is apparently successfully absorbed. Cambodia remains a disputed ground for guerrillas, and Laos is run by the Vietnamese Army.

The Chinese are not immune from unrest. Their government is experiencing the difficulties that come with relaxing controls and raising expectations that cannot easily be fulfilled. In North Korea, with its

The military coups in Fiji in May and September 1987 – which resulted in its expulsion from the Commonwealth – stemmed from fears of power going to the Indian community rather than the ethnic Melanesians. This occurrence is the first, but unlikely to be the last, of its kind in Oceana.

The current major flash-point between states is undoubtedly the South China Sea, where control of the Paracel and Spratley islands is in dispute. The adoption of 200-mile (322-km) economic exclusion zones, along with mineral rights on adjoining continental shelves, has resulted in renewed interest in any island on which a flag can be planted.

The Chinese, with their experience of oil in the Yellow Sea, seized bases in the Paracels from the South Vietnamese after bitterly fought naval actions in 1974. The Taiwanese also own some of the Paracels, as do the Philippines. In the Spratley group, several hundred miles farther south, the major power is the Vietnamese, but China, the Philippines, Malaysia and Indonesia all have an interest. The expansion of the Chinese Navy makes it likely that China will try to become even more dominant in this area.

To the north, China's border with the USSR is

US military involvement in the Pacific is immense. The two main forces are the 7th US Fleet in the western Pacific and the 3rd US Fleet in the east. Frequent exercises are carried out, alone and with allies.
Above: Tanks of the Blue Forces move up a mountain road in Korea to reach position for the start of joint services exercise Team Spirit.
Right: Thai and US forces in joint service exercise Cobra Gold 88.
Left: Japanese and US pilots inspect the F-15.

extremely rigid controls, it is arguable whether the regime will survive the death or overthrow of the long-serving Kim Il Sung, and South Korea has its own difficulties with an unpopular military regime.

Internally, there are problems in the French islands and in Fiji. All the French islands have independence movements, the most important of which is the FLNKS (Kanak Socialist National Liberation Front) of New Caledonia. A colony since 1853 and granted autonomous status in 1975, New Caledonia's nickel and chrome are too valuable, and the colonists too powerful, for the French metropolitan government to respond to demands for independence.

approaching stability. After the armed clashes on the Amur in 1969 there was a decade of relative calm, but there were more incidents in 1979 and neither side has completely accepted the other's position. President Gobarchev's visit to China in May 1989, during which he called for improved relations, may bring stability.

The USSR is also in dispute with Japan over the northern islands it seized in 1945. Japan has never accepted their loss, and wants to recover at least Shikotan and the Habomis off Hokkaido, which were never previously claimed by the USSR. Due to these differences, a peace treaty has yet to be signed between the two countries concerning World War II.

Above: A P36 Orion of the Royal Australian Air Force. With New Zealand's expulsion from the ANZUS treaty, Australia enjoys even closer ties with the USA.

A third problem for the USSR is the spectacular growth of South Korea, which cuts across its Pacific Fleet's route to the south. Relations sank to a new low following the shooting down of KAL 007 (a Boeing 747 airliner belonging to Korean Airlines) on September 5 1983 by a Soviet Sukhoi Su-15 Flagon fighter. The airliner had passed over a number of Soviet military installations, including the main nuclear submarine base at Petropavlovsk on the Kamchakta peninsular.

Decolonizaton

Independence dates:
    1945 Korea (N&S)
    1946 Philippines
    1948 Burma
    1949 Indonesia
    1954 Cambodia, Vietnam (N&S), Laos
    1957 Malaya
    1962 Western Samoa
    1963 Irian Jaya (West Irian to Indonesia), Sabah,
        Sarawak
    1965 Singapore
    1968 Nauru
    1970 Fiji, Tonga
    1975 Papua New Guinea
    1976 East Timor
    1978 Solomon Islands, Tuvalu
    1979 Kiribati
    1980 Vanuatu
    1985 Brunei
    1988 Cook Island, Nuie

Realignments

The most dramatic realignment has been that between China and the USA. By the end of the 1960s, both countries were ready to start talking after two decades of implacable hostility. China was worried about the Soviet military build-up near the northern frontier, and its own badly equipped and organized armed forces.

Nixon went to China in February 1972, and relations gradually improved to the point where, for example, the USA has replaced its Iranian electronic listening stations by ones in China and US arms manufacturers are improving Chinese weapons systems. An early by-product was the replacement of Taiwan by China in the UN (including the Security Council) in October 1971.

US involvement in Taiwan has gradually been whittled down. When the USA signed a treaty with China on

January 1 1979, it cancelled its 1955 defence pact with Taiwan. This was followed on August 17 1982 by the Shanghai Communique, by which the USA agreed to taper off its arms sales to Taiwan. Any semblance of political maturity disappeared in May and June of 1989, when the massacre by the army of thousands of unarmed students met with abhorrence world-wide, and the USA called a halt to arms sales to China. The storming of Tiananmen Square in Beijing, followed by the repression, has cast a blight over China's international relations. China and the Chinese market are too important for the USA to ignore for long, but the partial embargo on arms sale and development must delay the modernization of China's armed forces.

Another difficulty highlighted by the violent suppression of the moves to liberalism concerns Hong Kong. The inhabitants of Hong Kong have always been sceptical of the value of British and Chinese promises about maintaining important features of Hong Kong's 'separateness' after 1997. The Chinese upheavals and the lack of concern by Chinese leaders to international opinion have made most of Hong Kong's six million inhabitants extremely fearful for the future. Over the next few years they will exert much greater pressure on Britain to secure their future properly.

A major realignment has come about as a result of the worries of the south Pacific states over years of nuclear testing in the area, particularly in recent years by France. As early as 1973, Australia and New Zealand sent naval vessels to the French test zone at Mururoa

Below: Vietnamese refugees in 1975 occupy a landing craft in the South China Sea. The craft is transporting them to the Merchant Marine Ship *Transcolorado*.

Current Force Levels – Major Regional Powers

Australia – Over 70,000 men, more than 100 main battle tanks, 6 submarines, 12 major warships, 18 bombers, 70 fighter/attack aircraft.

China – Over 2.5 million men, about 12,000 main battle tanks, 53 major surface warships, almost 120 submarines, over 1,000 bombers and attack aircraft, about 4,000 fighters.

Indonesia – Nearly 300,000 men, no main battle tanks, 16 major warships, more than 40 attack aircraft, 14 fighters.

Japan – Nearly 250,000 men, about 1,200 main battle tanks, 54 major surface warships, 15 submarines, nearly 80 attack aircraft, 220 fighters.

Thailand – Over 250,000 men, 90 main battle tanks, 8 major surface warships, more than 40 attack aircraft, 30 fighters.

USA (Pacific only) – Over 30,000 ground troops, 8 SSBN and 40 SSN submarines, more than 100 major surface warships (including 6 carriers and 2 battleships), one B-52 bomber wing, over 200 fighter/attack aircraft. The USA has major troop and aircraft reinforcements readily deployable from continental USA.

USSR (Far Eastern theatre only) – About 400 ICBMs and over 170 IRBMs, about 56 divisions, more than 30 SSBN, about 80 SSGN/SSG and SSN/SS submarines, over 80 major surface warships (including 2 carriers and a battle cruiser), about 170 bombers, 360 attack aircraft and over 200 fighters.

Vietnam – Over 1.2 million men, about 1,600 main battle tanks, 7 major surface vessels, over 70 attack aircraft, over 200 fighters.

to protest about continued testing. On August 6 1985 eight states of the South Pacific Forum, including Australia and New Zealand, adopted the South Pacific Nuclear Free Zone Treaty. Both Australia and New Zealand had confrontations with Britain and the USA over whether their visiting warships carried nuclear weapons (neither ever say), and New Zealand persisted to the point where it was expelled from the ANZUS treaty in August 1986. Its attitude was strengthened by the sinking of the Greenpeace protest vessel *Rainbow Warrior* in Auckland Harbour by agents of the French intelligence service DGSE.

Chapter 3

HARDWARE:
Stealth technology

Like supersonic fighter aircraft in the 1960s, 'stealth' has become the 'buzz' military technology for the 1980s and beyond. Enormously impressive when employed in programmes such as the US B-2 strategic bomber, the technology is rapidly being applied to all aspects of warfare and to many kinds of war-fighting equipment. Accordingly, the press abounds with references to the various applications; there are stories that are full of strange-sounding acronyms – stories that invest the almost inevitably 'super secret' projects to which stealth technology has been applied with magical properties. The reality is perhaps more mundane but infinitely more interesting.

The roll-out of the Northrop B-2 – the USAF's Advanced Strategic Bomber. The B-2 is the first truly all-stealth bomber. It is a composite flying wing, designed with the aid of a three-dimensional computer database to minimize development costs.

Stealth or, more properly, 'low observability' techniques, is a direct result of the urgent need to restore the balance between offensive and defensive capabilities brought about by the huge strides made in sensor technology since the end of World War II. Such advances have resulted in detection and guidance systems of unprecedented accuracy and sensitivity, and have vastly increased the range of sensor types available. Whereas the combatants in World War II had four embryonic sensor technologies to aid them in solving the air defence problem, their counterparts today can call on upwards of a dozen fully developed, fully integrated techniques with levels of redundancy undreamt of 40 years ago. This new level of sophistication is not restricted to aerial warfare, the benefits and problems are just as spectacular at sea or on the land battlefield.

Stealth technology aims to suppress the system signatures (radar, heat, visual and acoustic) to the point where they are extremely difficult to detect. To be successful, the various sub-technologies have to be applied in the right mix to suit the particular requirement. Thus, the 'stealthy' bomber is designed to maximize the detection problem for the enemy and so enhance its own penetration capability. At sea, the 'stealthy' warship tries to make itself as difficult a target as possible for the sea-skimming missile. Beneath the waves, the 'stealthy' submarine is intended to run as quietly as possible to avoid sonar detection. On the land battlefield, the 'stealthy' installation is intended to deceive the new generation of airborne surveillance radars, which have detection ranges measured in hundreds of miles.

Defeating radar

Taking account of these various factors makes the technology and its application complex. Defeating radar detection is perhaps the most complex. A radar set finds its target by transmitting microwave energy into space and detecting any of that energy which is reflected from an object in its path. To defeat this process, stealth offers two techniques: signature management and Radar Absorbent Materials (RAMs).

RAM makes use of the energy-exchange properties of carbon and some magnetic iron (ferrite) compounds. When 'illuminated' by microwave energy, the molecular structure of these materials is excited (given an elevated energy band) and the excitation converts the received microwave energy into heat. In this way, the material absorbs the signal to the point where there is insufficient energy to create a sizeable echo signal.

Although this basic principle is simple, its implementation is vastly critical, especially in applications where material weight and ability to withstand stress are important factors. As the technology stands today, RAM materials can be broadly divided into four sub-categories: broad-band or genuine absorbers, narrow-band resonant absorbers, hybrid combinations of the two and surface paints.

Genuine absorbers offer a consistent performance over a range of microwave frequencies and can be used in shipboard and fixed-site applications. In the aerospace field, such materials are applicable where the RAM is integrated with the vehicle's structure rather than applied to it. Such an application might take the form of a honeycomb sandwich with radar-transparent 'skins' for strength and an internal cell structure in which the individual cell walls are coated with a rigid foam loaded with an absorber of carbon or ferrite. The foam is applied in such a way as to present a logarithmically graded resistance to the incoming signal. Another option is to make the sandwich filling an array of specially shaped absorbent foam pyramids.

The efficacy of such broad-band absorbers was demonstrated in the USA as early as the 1960s when studies showed that a 1-inch (25-mm) thick fibreglass-skinned honeycomb structure, using carbon black and

silver powder as the absorber, could achieve 95 per cent absorption against signals in the 2.5-13 GHz frequency range. Although the anti-radar performance of such a material was impressive, its weight and relative fragility precluded its use in the very important aerospace field, other than on subsonic airframes that need not be highly manoeuvrable. Today, these problems have been largely solved with the availability of skinning materials such as Kevlar and carbon-fibre which are as strong as steel.

The narrow-band or resonant absorbers offer the advantage of light weight but are only effective against a specific target frequency. Equally, their performance is dependent on the angle of incidence at which the microwave energy hits them. Most narrow-band materials work most efficiently if this relationship is a 90° angle, their effectiveness falling off dramatically at any value below 45°. Usually, these materials comprise an elastomer, such as rubber, loaded with an absorber and backed by a metallic reflecting sheet.

The material is tuned to its target signal by varying its depth which, ideally, should be a quarter of the wavelength of that signal. Suppression is achieved by the incoming signal being both absorbed and reflected through the material from the base layer. Some microwave energy will always escape from RAMs. In narrow-band materials, this escape is cancelled out by the material generating reflections equal in strength to the natural one. To the receiving radar, this quasi-optical technique denies it any chance of detecting the faint natural echo response.

Broader ranges of target frequencies can be dealt with by multi-layer applications in which each successive layer is targeted against its own specific frequency. Although narrow-band absorbers do have their limitations, their light weight, flexibility and ability to be applied to existing structures make them useful in a range of applications, particularly where there is a need to provide a defence against a specific type of radar.

Above and left: The SR-71 Blackbird reconnaissance aircraft, developed by Lockheed, exploited stealth design to the full. Blackbird incorporates radar-absorbing material in its surface, and its shape is contoured to eliminate right angles and give minimal radar cross-section. It flies at more than three times the speed of sound at altitudes in excess of 80,000 ft and holds the world air speed record, set by the USAF.

The Rockwell B-1B (with refuelling markers) uses low-observability or stealth technology to achieve a radar cross-section only 1 per cent that of a B-52.

The critical nature of signal angle of incidence to the narrow-band absorber seems to be one of the major driving forces behind the development of hybrid materials which exhibit characteristics of both broad- and narrow-band RAMs. Such combinations produce an absorption performance that peaks at certain angles but degrades less when the parameters are not the ideal.

The surface coating used in stealth technology is iron-ball paint. As its name implies, this is paint loaded with iron (ferrite) particles which is particularly effective in the suppression of signal re-emission induced by surface-current effects. When a structure is illuminated by a microwave signal, electrical currents are generated on any part of its surface that is conductive. This activity in turn generates a re-transmission effect which amplifies the radar's echo. The absorbent qualities of the iron in such paints goes a long way towards eliminating this unwelcome phenomenon.

Signature management

Together with the use of RAMs, signature management can give significant benefits. In the aerospace industry, for example, every warplane flying today has a Radar Cross Section (RCS), determined by the strength of the echo signal it reflects when illuminated by radar. The RCS value varies according to the geometric relationship between the aircraft and the radar emitter and can be significantly reduced if the shape of the aircraft is well-designed. Of particular importance are in-built corner reflectors inherent in the design.

Corner reflectors occur where any two or more surface planes come together at or near 90° to one another. So an aircraft that carries its engines on wing pylons has an RCS considerably greater than one with the power plants tucked into the wing roots, even though the two have similar overall dimensions. The

importance of this geometry lies in the relationship between RCS and detection performance: the bigger a target's RCS, the easier it is for the radar to find it. The RCS does not depend solely on external structure but is also heavily influenced, in the aerospace field particularly, by radar bright spots generated by such things as the compressor stages of turbojet engines.

The solutions to these problems have produced one of stealth technology's most overt manifestations – blended vehicle shaping. The US B-2 bomber demonstrates the principle well – it has no sharp surface junctions marring its flowing, almost organic lines. Closer examination shows the organic analogy to be not quite true because what is required is the elimination of all 90° junctions. Accordingly, the blending effect does not need to involve constant use of curves; flat planes will do equally well, provided they do not make the 90° junction with any other surface.

The validity of this concept is shown clearly in stealth shaping on warships, where overall RCS is markedly reduced by building the vessel's superstructure in such a way that surfaces that normally would be vertical and horizontal are in fact set at about 84°. Areas that cannot be treated in this manner, such as engine compressor stages, can be effectively masked if tunnels leading to them are snaked or fitted with baffles to hide and eliminate bright spots.

As well as reducing RCS, careful vehicle shaping can be used to re-direct radar echo signals away from the emitter's receiver. As early as the late 1950s, US scientists worked out that arranging an aircraft's exterior surfaces in such a way as to reflect any received radar energy at angles of about 20° above or below the emitter's horizon, would reduce its broadside RCS to a tenth of its untreated value. A prime example of this approach is to be seen in Lockheed's Goblin, the F-117A stealth fighter.

The degradation of radar performance is a major aspect of stealth, but it is by no means the only factor; the suppression of a vehicle's thermal, visual and aural signatures are just as important. Thermal suppression is particularly important in aerospace and naval applications to overcome the threat posed by heat-seeking missiles and infra-red detection and tracking systems.

In aerospace applications, the major source of thermal energy is the engine exhaust plume. This can be made less apparent in a number of ways, ranging from the use of non-afterburning jet engines, through directing the hot exhaust gases away from the infra-red seeker's field of view to shielding the exhaust ports and mixing the efflux with the colder passing airflow prior to discharge. The threat posed by infra-red detection systems should not be underestimated, a fact recently demonstrated by work being done at the UK's Royal Aircraft Establishment which has shown that with computer enhancement, aircraft types can clearly be identified by their thermal signatures at long ranges. The microwave-to-heat energy exchange inherent in

RAM may pose interesting problems in this respect.

Recent advances in electro-optic weapons guidance systems make a vehicle's visual signature an important consideration. In current aerospace stealth applications, small is beautiful. Northrop's B-2 bomber is small when viewed from particular angles and when compared with its predecessors. To a closing head-on interceptor pilot, there is a lot less to see of a B-2 than a B-52.

The suppression of visual signature goes beyond mere size. For example, the way in which the vehicle is painted can greatly affect its visual signature. A visit to any current military airshow will demonstrate how effective camouflage paint can be. If further evidence of this is required, one need look no further than an incident in the mid-1980s when an RAF Jaguar pilot flew into a USAF A-10 during an exercise because he simply could not differentiate the aircraft from its background, so good was its camouflage.

The effectiveness of camouflage paint does not stop at the ability to blend in with the surroundings. Recent developments include pigments incorporated into the surface finish which will not respond to, say, infra-red

Right: The B-52 is highly observable not only to the unaided eye, but to enemy radar and infra-red sensors. The reflective surfaces and hot engine exhaust make the B-52 a large target. The A-10 Thunderbolt (below) is not a stealth aircraft but it presents a small infra-red image and can be camouflaged well.

Above: Four F-18A Hornets from Canada's Night Hawk Squadron with false canopies painted on the undersides. The use of camouflage to confuse and disorientate opponents is part of the stealth concept. When the aircraft manoeuvres (below) during dogfights, enemy pilots can misinterpret which way up it is flying.

illumination. Equally, camouflage can be used not to make a craft invisible but to disorientate an opponent, a technique developed by the US Navy during the 1970s and seen today on Canada's F/A-18 aircraft. Close examination of such planes shows a false canopy painted on the lower fuselage beneath the real thing. This is intended to give the pilot the edge in a dog fight, winning vital manoeuvring freedom as his opponent tries to figure out which way up the camouflaged aircraft is flying. Thinking he is looking down on his target may lead him to anticipate the wrong manoeuvres.

Acoustic suppression is primarily of interest in sub-surface warfare and is intended to combat the sonar threat to submarines. Such shielding takes the form of tiles applied to a particular boat's hull and sail. The physical properties of these sound-absorbent materials remain unclear, so heavily classified are such programmes in the West. From the available evidence they appear to be elastomer-based and could make use of an internal pyramidal structure in which the sound energy is attenuated or diminished as it bounces back and forth between the various surfaces. Photographs of British and Soviet submarines treated in this way suggest that they have the same problems as the Space Shuttle – the tiles drop off during operational missions.

Operational strategies

Alongside these specific stealth measures, the technology as a whole depends as much on operational strategies as anything else. A decision has to be made as to what exactly the stealth features incorporated into a system are intended to achieve. In designing a penetration bomber, for example, the requirement is to avoid detection for as long as possible and to make the interception task as difficult as possible. In the design of a mine-hunter, the need is not so much to avoid detection from the surface or air as to evade the detection sensors on underwater weapons.

The incorporated stealth features are of little use if they are compromised by electro-magnetic emissions from the particular vehicle. The importance of passive listening devices to modern military doctrine cannot be overemphasized. Any transmission, be it a navigational radar or a communications signal, can and will be exploited by an enemy. Accordingly, to be effective, the stealth platform has to operate in conditions of virtual radio/radar silence. This presents problems, particularly for the operation of avionic nav/attack systems which are essentially 'active' in function. The use of the latest satellite navigation systems and the new low-power, 'quiet' radars goes some way towards solving these problems but the strict control of any form of active transmission is crucial to the stealth concept.

Just as important as this control of intentional transmissions, care must be taken to mask the natural radiation generated by onboard systems. Even if a radar set is in standby mode – powered up but not actually transmitting – it will generate both microwave and heat energy, both of which must be hidden from external detectors. The mission profile and the threat likely to be encountered will determine the stealth features

used. If for instance, a vehicle is likely to encounter threats from the front and above, the stealth features must be designed to cover those specific quadrants. Less vulnerable quarters may be left less protected, with the consequent advantages of reduction in weight and cost. If the type of threat to be encountered is known with any precision, protection from other segments can safely be left out. Successful stealth is achieved by using the right combination of specialized technologies together with the operational doctrines necessary to secure a specific mission objective.

The first attempts at a form of stealth came in the period 1914-1935 when first German and then Soviet aircraft designers tried to produce aircraft that were difficult to see. The Soviet attempt centred on the work of S. G. Kozlov who modified a Yakovlev AIR-4 monoplane into a 'Nyevidimyi Samolyet' – invisible aeroplane. The modifications involved stripping the aircraft of its original fabric covering, painting the internal structure white and then re-covering the airframe with a transparent material called Rodoid. Trials with the aeroplane showed that indeed it was difficult to spot visually, but it could still be heard. And although the aircraft skin and structure could be made to appear transparent, features such as engines, fuel tanks, tyres and pilots could not. The project died.

The development of radar itself established the principles behind RAM. The first practical application of the technique was made by the German Navy's U-Boat arm during World War II. Having established the existence of Allied S-band ASV radar, the Germans began to apply two kinds of RAM – Jaumann and Wesch-Mat – to the sails of their submarines to evade detection while the boats were travelling on the surface. Jaumann comprised a covering made of seven thin layers of semi-conducting material, separated from one another by dielectric layers of equal thickness. The semi-conducting layers were manufactured from lamp-black (carbon) impregnated paper which was about 0.004 inch (0.1 mm) thick. The actual microwave absorption was achieved by exponentially graduating the conductivity of the various layers in the sandwich.

Wesch-Mat, on the other hand, was a twin-layer material, the outer of which was a waffle-shaped moulding made of a rubber-like elastomer loaded with carbonyl iron powder. Behind this was a 0.04-inch (1-mm) thick rubber backing sheet, the two together having an overall thickness of about 0.3 inch (7.6 mm). The records are incomplete but Wesch-Mat at least is said to have been an effective RAM against the 3-cm and 10-cm radars used by the Allied air forces for submarine hunting.

German mistakes about the switch-over from metric to centimetric radars for submarine detection, and

Left: Missing tiles of radar-absorbing material from a Typhoon-class Soviet Navy submarine indicate the use of stealth technology to avoid detection by aircraft.

their belief in the existence of an infra-red sensor system, appear to have led to the development of anti-infra-red paints designed to defeat active equipment by responding poorly to illumination at the red end of the electromagnetic spectrum.

On the other hand, considerable argument raged within the RAF as to what the best form of aircraft camouflage would be to reduce the distances at which they could be spotted by the crew of a surfaced U-boat. Preliminary calculations postulated that for the weather conditions around northern Europe and in the Atlantic, a white-painted aeroplane could probably get 20 per cent nearer a target U-boat without detection than one painted in any other colour. Once this concept of minimizing the visual contrast between an aeroplane and its sky background was established, ways were sought to improve on the figure quoted.

One of the first ideas put forward was to coat the aircraft in a reflective white finish made up of small prisms. Operating in the same way as the 'cat's eyes' on roads, they were to be configured to reflect the available light down towards the surface of the sea. This scheme was dropped when researchers realised that in direct sunlight the finish would significantly increase the aircraft's visibility.

In 1941, attention turned to 'light camouflage' in which the aircraft was to be artificially lit to eliminate the contrast between it and the sky. Initial thinking suggested flood lighting the aircraft's flanks and lower

surfaces but calculations quickly showed that this would be prohibitively expensive in terms of power consumption. Attention then turned to illuminating the aircraft's nose and wing leading edges only, a sensible suggestion bearing in mind the angle from which the U-Boat crew would most frequently first see the attacking aircraft.

Considerable effort was put into the project by the RAF but problems with power consumption and equipment drag prolonged the development period sufficiently for it not to see operational service. The Americans also took an interest in the concept and under the codename 'Yahoody', developed their own version of it. The British system aimed at providing cover over 90° in azimuth and 20° in elevation, whereas Yahoody was limited to 9° cover in both planes. Like the British effort, US work in the field failed to produce an operational application by the close of hostilities.

The close of hostilities in 1945 saw the principles of stealth well established. Indeed, the Germans had by accident produced a highly effective stealth fighter – the Gotha Go 229.

The Gotha prototype was an extremely stealthy 'beast', although low observability probably played little part in the design process – Germany's need being for high-performance jet fighters to combat the aerial assault being waged against it by the Allied air forces. Essentially a 55-ft (16.8-m) span flying wing, the

For a new military technology, stealth has a surprisingly long history, dating back to German attempts to produce invisible aircraft in 1914. In the years after World War II, the US company, Northrop, continued to develop the concept with its 'flying wings'. The YB-49 (left) was the world's largest and longest-ranging jet bomber, and was a development of the piston-engined XB-35 (below left). The N9M (below) was a scaled model of the B-35 used in the design and testing of the aircraft.

Go 229 featured concealed engines, a clean, well-blended shape and a small frontal area – all excellent stealth features. Furthermore, the aircraft's wooden structure made radar detection difficult – a phenomenon the Germans themselves had already encountered in trying to track the RAF's Mosquito. The prototype Go 229 made its maiden flight during the summer of 1944 and it may be significant for the overall stealth story that the Americans captured the partly completed

third prototype in 1945 and shipped it to the USA for evaluation.

The same pattern of accidental stealth continued in the post-war world with the emergence of Northrop's YB-35 and YB-49 flying wing strategic bombers. The piston-engined YB-35 came within an ace of entering serial production, eventually losing out in a political battle which led to the introduction of Convair's more conventional B-36. The B-35 was followed in 1947 by the jet-powered B-49 but again, the type did not go into production. It is doubly ironic that the USA's first true stealth bomber, the B-2, is essentially a Northrop design and the USAF could have had such a plane in service perhaps as much as 30 years earlier.

The late 1950s saw the real beginnings of today's stealth programmes. By this time, it had become clear that the manned bomber as the primary means of nuclear weapons delivery was becoming too vulnerable. Improvements in Soviet defence technology had forced the West's nuclear bombers 'into the weeds' by the mid-1960s and turned the strategic planners' attention towards submarine-launched missiles as the primary instrument of the aptly named Mutually Assured Destruction (MAD) doctrine of deterrence. It was at this low point for aerial delivery systems that work on the first of today's generation of stealth aircraft, Lockheed's SR-71 Blackbird, began.

Work on this truly remarkable aeroplane can be traced back to October 1955 when the California-based Garrett Corporation received a USAF contract for studies into a liquid-oxygen aircraft engine (based on a concept developed by a British engineer, Randolph Rae) and an airframe for it to power. Being primarily an engine manufacturer, Garrett sub-contracted the airframe design to Lockheed. When work was stopped on the engine programme in October 1957, Lockheed continued work on what had now become plans for a Mach 3 plus reconnaissance aircraft. During 1958/59, the company's famous 'Skunk Works' special projects facility drafted 12 separate proposals, designated A-1 to -12, the last of which was awarded a development contract in August 1959.

Here is not the place to record the story of the CIA's A-12 and the USAF's SR-71 which was developed from it. What is germane to this story is the fact that both aircraft featured stealth shaping and, perhaps more importantly, were among the first operational vehicles to incorporate RAM materials as an integral part of their structures. According to one noted authority on the subject, both the A-12 and the SR-71 use two types of RAM: iron-ball paint and a plastic honeycomb material specially developed for the job by Lockheed. The plastic RAM is used on the leading and trailing edges of the A-12's and the SR-71's wings, and it forms the major constructional element on the 'chines' mounted along the sides of the A-12's forwards fuselage.

In the SR-71 (the A-12 no longer being in service), the plastic RAM is applied in the form of v-shaped

wedges let into the primary titanium wing structure. Incoming microwave energy enters the shapes and in travelling back and forth across them, is progressively absorbed. Perhaps the most remarkable aspect of this application was, and indeed is, the fact that this specially developed material can withstand 316°C (600°F) skin temperatures without melting.

With the advent of the A-12/SR-71 programme, the stealth story becomes fragmentary due to the extremely high levels of classification placed on the technology and the vehicles using it. The successes achieved in the Blackbird programme seem to have led to a range of US stealth studies, the details of which are unclear.

The next confirmed manifestation of the technology appears during the 1960s when some form of RAM appears to have been applied to reconnaissance drones used in Vietnam. Photographs of Teledyne Ryan's Model 147T drone suggest strongly that this vehicle utilized either structural or parasitic RAMs throughout its airframe, especially the wings, nose and tail surfaces. Other drone types from this company also exhibit the use of RAM 'blankets' covering vulnerable airframe components as well as mesh engine intake grills to deflect radar energy from the front end of the vehicle's jet engine.

Stealth drone design reached a peak in the late 1960s when the US Compass Arrow reconnaissance programme produced the AMQ-91A vehicle which was used operationally in the Far East until the Sino-US accords terminated operations in 1973. AMQ-91 featured extensive use of RAM in its structure and shape to achieve low observability. Thermal signature suppression was handled by mounting the vehicle's engine on the top of the fuselage and shielding the exhaust efflux with two canted vertical tail surfaces.

The conflict in SE Asia also produced aircraft like Lockheed's QT-2 and YO-3 platforms, which addressed the problem of acoustic suppression. The need to locate hostile forces in the jungles of Vietnam and its immediate neighbours led to Lockheed Missile & Space Co being awarded a contract during 1966 for the development of an ultra-quiet reconnaissance aircraft which could operate a payload of short-range, high-technology sensors effectively. Using the two-seat Schweizer X-26A sailplane as a base, Lockheed developed the QT (Quiet Thruster) -2 vehicle which was powered by a specially muffled 100-hp (75-kW) Continental 0-200-A air-cooled engine driving a low-speed, four-bladed wooden propeller.

The prototype QT-2 made its maiden flight during July 1967 and a test programme rapidly established that it was so quiet as to be virtually undetectable. This aircraft and one other, now known as QT-2PCs ('PC'

Left: Pilots of the SR-71 Blackbird and the TR-1 reconnaissance aircraft wear a full pressure suit to protect them in the event of cabin decompression at the extremely high altitude of their missions.

Stealth Cruise Missile

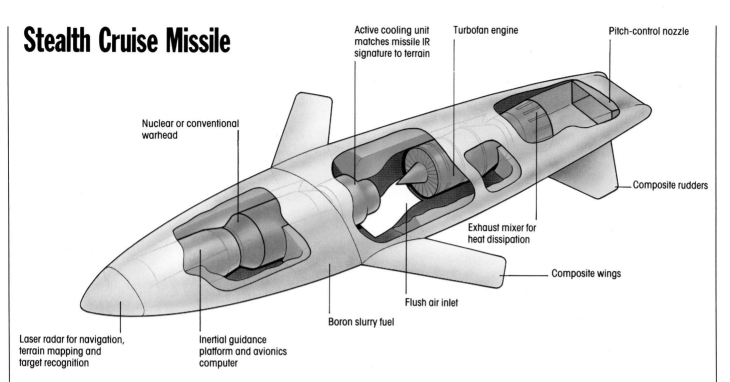

Active cooling unit matches missile IR signature to terrain

Turbofan engine

Pitch-control nozzle

Nuclear or conventional warhead

Composite rudders

Exhaust mixer for heat dissipation

Composite wings

Flush air inlet

Boron slurry fuel

Laser radar for navigation, terrain mapping and target recognition

Inertial guidance platform and avionics computer

for 'Prize Crew', the programme codename) were shipped to Vietnam, arriving in December 1967. The success of the Prize Crew aircraft led to Lockheed being awarded a second contract for 14 YO-3 aircraft in July 1968. The YO-3 was a more extensive modification of the X-26A, featuring a revised undercarriage, a new cockpit canopy and a 210-hp (158-kW) Continental IO-360D engine driving a six-bladed, fixed-pitch propeller. Thirteen YO-3s were shipped to Vietnam early in 1970 and were used operationally by the US Army's 1st Army Security Agency Company, based at Long Binh in South Vietnam. The unit was eventually withdrawn in April 1972 and two of its aircraft are currently operated by the Louisiana Department of Wildlife and Fisheries to track down poachers in its game reserves.

As the SE Asian conflict was ending, the 'Skunk Works' was busily working on new stealth studies. At roughly the same time, Dr Leo Windecker was interesting the USAF in his work on non-metallic low RCS aircraft using the new breed of composite materials for their construction. In 1972 or thereabouts, Windecker received a contract to build a low RCS prototype, the YE-5A, based on his ideas. The aircraft was delivered to the service the following year and was used in a wide range of classified tests.

The general work seems to have been encompassed in the overall 'Have Blue' programme which culminated in Boeing, Grumman, McDonnell Douglas and Lockheed being asked for proposals for a proof-of-concept stealth demonstrator. Of these companies, the submissions from Grumman and Lockheed were adjudged to be the most promising, Lockheed winning out with a 1976 contract to build five prototype demonstrators. The first of these aircraft made its maiden flight during 1977 and the programme led directly to the current F-117A stealth fighters.

Above: The AGM-129A is a stealth successor to the US air-launched cruise missile. The 129A is thought to be able to fly by body lift alone, any wings being jettisoned before the final attack.

The other strand of the current USAF stealth programme, Northrop's B-2 bomber, seems to have had its genesis in a 1980 Presidential decision to leapfrog the existing B-1 and proceed with a full-blown 'low-observability penetration' aircraft. Press reports suggested that 'requests for proposals' for such an aircraft were issued to two teams of contractors – Lockheed/Rockwell and Northrop/Boeing – during 1981. From the available information, the Lockheed/Rockwell submission may have been a scaled-up F-117, although this is by no means certain. In the event, the Northrop/ Boeing design won the day and it has been suggested that a sub-scale, proof-of-concept vehicle was first flown during 1982. The prototype B-2 was rolled out on November 22 1988 and is expected to make its first flight this year.

In a parallel programme to the B-2, General Dynamics developed a stealthy successor to the existing air-launched cruise missile, the AGM-129A. The release of the first photograph of this weapon revealed that it is probably a wingless, lifting body incorporating both RAM and signal-management shaping to avoid detection. Power is provided by a Williams International F112 turbojet fed by a flush air intake. Informed sources suggest that the vehicle's tail surfaces form an inverted V, providing shielding for the engine's exhaust. Guidance appears to be by means of terrain-matching in concert with a low-probability-of-intercept active altitude sensor. The USAF may eventually receive as many as 2,000 of these weapons which will initially be carried by B-52H and then B-1B aircraft.

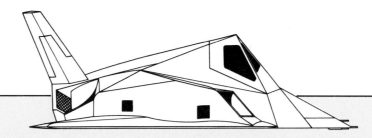

The Lockheed F-117A Stealth Fighter

Lockheed's goblin-like F-117A stealth fighter is believed to have made its maiden flight in June 1981. It is now operational with the USAF's 4450th Tactical Group, based at Tonopah airfield in Nevada, and the USAF plans to procure 59 such aircraft.

As far as can be ascertained from the single officially released photograph, the F-117A has a wing span of approximately 38 ft (11.6 m) and overall length of 24-26 ft (7.3-7.9 m). Fuselage width is about 10 ft (3 m) and overall height is reported to be 12-16 ft (3.7-4.9 m). Power is provided by two General Electric F404 non-afterburning turbofans, giving the aircraft a purely subsonic performance. The overall design seems to be intended to deflect rather than absorb microwave energy, especially from the front and above. This is strongly suggestive of a low-level role. Because signal deflection is a major factor of the design, the use of RAM in its construction is highly likely.

Landing is accomplished on a conventional tricycle undercarriage and the aircraft's undersurfaces are reported to be virtually flat; indeed the design has some of the characteristics of a lifting body. No clear details of the type of intake configuration are available (this area having been heavily censored in the available illustration)

but they may be expected to be of an unconventional kind. The two turbofans appear to exhaust from broad, square nozzles over the rear fuselage. The canted vertical tail surfaces (each with moving control surfaces fore and aft) provide thermal masking from above and it may be that the exhaust efflux is cooled by passing through a baffle system.

The F-117A is air transportable by C-5 aircraft, so the wings and vertical tail surfaces fold or are dismantled for loading. Armament is likely to be restricted to single AGM-65 or AGM-88 missiles, carried in an internal 15-ft (4.5-m) long weapons bay. An alternative to this might be conformal racks which would increase the weapons lift considerably. Navigation is thought to be by means of the Navstar global positioning system and any attack sensors carried by the aircraft are thought to be passive. It may be significant that the F-117A will fit the elevators on any of the USN's current carriers, and the *New York Times* has reported that the type has already been temporarily deployed at a UK airbase and that Oliver North proposed the type for a strike on Libya. The true identity of the F-117A is confused by the publication of unofficial photographs in the American journal *Aviation Week & Space Technology*, dated

May 1 1989. According to this source, groups of between six and ten F-117As have been spotted in daylight flying over the Mojave Desert in California during April 1989. The plan view photographs accompanying the article, although poor in quality, show a distinctly different aircraft from that shown in the official release.

The Mk 2 F-117A appears to be 45 ft (3.7 m) long with a wing span of 39 ft (11.8 m) and a wing leading edge sweep angle of about 58 degrees. The aircraft's length and wing sweep angle are significantly different from those of the Mk 1. Furthermore, the Mk 2's rear fuselage geometry incorporates a saw-tooth wing trailing edge configuration, rather than the squared-off format used on the Mk 1. The two aircraft have different tail-plane geometries, the Mk 2 featuring what appear to be separate v-shaped horizontal stabilizers.

Given the poor quality of all F-117A photographs so far available, it is extremely difficult to draw any definite conclusions about the true identity of the F-117A. Most probably, however, the USAF's official release actually shows a prototype and the later *Aviation Week* photographs depict the production standard aircraft.

The highly classified and mysterious F-117A stealth fighter has been shown to the world only as ghost-like indistinct images.

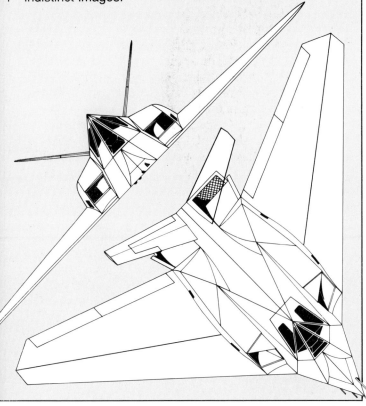

Stealth technology is being taken up with some urgency in the design of warships. The loss of *HMS Sheffield* during the 1982 Falklands/Malvinas conflict and damaging of the *USS Stark* during operations in the Gulf, have convinced naval planners that the existing defences against sea-skimming missiles are not sufficiently effective. Both these vessels were equipped with sophisticated, passive receptors which should have provided sufficient warning to activate countermeasures against the incoming round. In the *Sheffield*, this equipment was apparently disrupted by the simultaneous use of the vessel's satellite communications facilities, and on the *Stark* the equipment seemed to have provided incorrect data or data which were incorrectly understood. Either way, the world's deep-water navies cannot afford to lose such vessels to a relatively simple missile armed with a 360-lb (165-kg) warhead.

One solution to this problem is stealth shaping to reduce the vessels' RCS and make it less detectable to the radar seeker aboard an incoming missile. The right mix of stealth shaping and electronic countermeasures, such as chaff or active decoys, seems to be the best solution. Perhaps the Soviet Navy has taken this concept more seriously than its Western counterparts, with vessels such as the big Kirov-class cruisers offering an RCS about one-third the size of that of the much smaller Royal Navy Type 21 ASW frigate. The UK's new Type 23 vessels are being built along stealth lines with off-true superstructure surfaces and curved deck edges, as are, it is believed, a number of Japanese vessels. US concept drawings show stealth design taken to its logical conclusion, with warships comprising virtually nothing but a hull, the lines of which are broken only by a small wheelhouse. Armament is expected to comprise enclosed missile-launching tubes.

On the land battlefield, attention is turning towards ways of defeating the latest generation of airborne surveillance radars capable of penetrating hundreds of miles behind the front line. Besides tracking mobile tank formations, these systems will undoubtedly be used to locate high-value fixed targets such as airfields, command posts, and stores dumps. UK manufacturer Woodville Polymers has proposed using stealth technology to hide such installations. For airfields, the company suggests RAM curtains to mask the radar returns from the blast doors of hangars and hardened shelters, a radar reflecting netting for covering individual aircraft and ground equipment, including radar reflectors, tuned to give, say, the same response as an aircraft and which are located away from the base to lure attackers away from the real targets. Masking features such as runways, which show up extremely well on some types of radars, is more difficult but might be accomplished by using some form of durable RAM matting.

Stealth technology is undoubtedly a fascinating branch of military science but, despite its successes, there remains one big question mark – its viability. In sea and land applications it certainly is viable. An evaluation of its airborne applications gives a less certain response. Given the Soviet Union's capabilities and the likely scenarios in the event of a crisis, it is difficult to see the value of about 50 F-117As. Equally, the size and subsonic performance of the B-2 indicate strongly that the aircraft must be targeted at a specific 'window of opportunity' within the Soviet defensive network. The Soviets have evolved a multi-layered, multi-system air defence organization to defend their territory. To defeat such a system, the B-2 will have to operate at the precise altitude where the various systems and sensors provide the least effective cover, a condition requiring a level of prior intelligence which is enormously costly to achieve.

Experts are suggesting that over-the-horizon and bistatic sensing (transmitting from one point and receiving from a number of others) could effectively detect stealth vehicles. On the political level, other analysts suggest strongly that the availability of such a weapon as the B-2 will destabilize the US-Soviet equilibrium and generate a new arms race as the Soviets strive to reach parity with the US capability. It is perhaps significant that, so far, the Soviet Union seems to have done little work on stealth aircraft other than for reconnaissance.

Whatever else stealth does, it will inevitably generate a revolution in sensor technology. Already, the Soviet Union is believed to be developing new types of submarine detection systems, including surface signature sensors to record the disturbance to the sea's surface caused by a passing submarine, sensors to detect chemical and radioactive contamination and new types of electrical and magnetic systems to sense the changes in the Earth's magnetic field caused by submarines. Similar types of non-traditional sensors are bound to be developed for aerial warfare, plunging the world once more into massive military spending.

The stealth concept goes beyond aerospace applications. For example, the Soviet Navy has made great advances in making its Kirov-class cruisers (below) less vulnerable to attack from sea-skimming missiles.

The Northrop B-2 Stealth Bomber

Northrop's B-2 strategic stealth bomber is an all composite 'flying-wing' design with a span of 172 ft (52.4 m), a length of 69 ft (21.03 m) and a height of 17 ft (5.18 m). Power is provided by four General Electric F-118-GE-100 un-reheated turbofans, giving the aircraft a high subsonic performance. Combat radius is thought to be more than 5,000 miles (8,045 km). The design is highly innovative and different from that adapted for Northrop's earlier 'flying wings', the YB-35 and YB-47. This is as much a reflection of advances in flight control techniques as anything else.

Large-scale use is made of RAMs throughout the aircraft's structure and its four over-wing, partly 'buried' engine installations can be expected to offer thermal-signature suppression. Of particular note are the saw-toothed engine intakes (designed to mask the engines from microwave illumination) and the jagged trailing edge configuration. Flight control appears to be vested in outboard flap/elevon surfaces and inboard thrust-vector flaps positioned directly behind the engine intakes. The use of two types of control system can be expected: fly-by-wire/fly-by-light to help smooth out control difficulties inherent in the overall design, and gust control to help damp out the flexing movements likely in such a large composite structure.

The aircraft's crew complement is reported to be two and there is evidence of a Hughes 'covert strike' radar with two antenna arrays mounted left and right below the cockpit area. Some authorities believe there may be provision for a third crew member. Estimates place the aircraft's warload at approximately 40,000 lb (18,000 kg), made up of 16 SRAM II missiles or B83 free-fall nuclear bombs. Both types of weapon are packed in eight-round rotary launchers carried internally.

Other avionic systems carried by the aircraft are believed to be a Sanders passive defensive receiver system, a thermal imager, a Honeywell low-probability-of-intercept radar altimeter and a Kearfott navigation system to cue the SRAM II missiles. Other equipment probably includes the Navstar global positioning system.

The B-2 was expected to make its maiden flight approximately two months after roll out (November 1988). This flight was made in July 1989. In the current budgetry climate, a price tag of $500 million each may mean that production will be spread over a longer period. The first 34 aircraft will be stationed at Whiteman AFB, Missouri, and the USAF may procure as many as 132 of the type.

Northrop have used a three-dimensional computer database to design and build the B-2 and its prototypes (five in all) are being produced as production airframes.

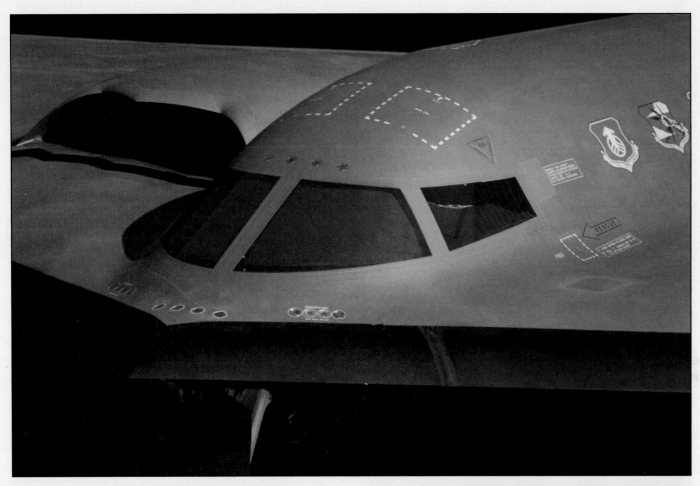

The USAF's B-2 stealth bomber is the culmination of Northrop's experiments with 'flying-wings' over four decades. The B-2's engine intakes and cockpit canopy are blended into the wing, and the intakes are saw-tooth shaped (above). It has neither vertical nor horizontal surfaces (right), and the engines are completely shielded (below) within the airframe. These details, together with the use of radar-absorbing materials, make the B-2 virtually invisible to radar, infra-red and other sensors. The B-2 is a challenge to sensor developers.

Chapter 4
CONFLICT:
Afghanistan

The Red Army invaded Afghanistan on Christmas Eve 1979. They moved with speed and efficiency, drawing on their experiences in Czechoslovakia and Hungary. Within a week the Soviets had nearly 50,000 troops inside Afghanistan. They were well-pleased with their coup. It had all gone smoothly. Their man was in charge, their troops were in position and Western powers, although furious, seemed impotent. But this was the start of a war which was to last nine years, cost the lives of 13,310 Russian soldiers (according to Soviet figures), cause destruction to Afghanistan, seriously harm the Soviet Union's international standing and, in President Gorbachev's words, became the Soviet Union's 'bleeding wound'.

Soviet troops returning from the war in Afghanistan arrive at Termez, a Soviet town near the border with Afghanistan. The Soviets maintained that they made an orderly withdrawal, unlike the Americans, who scrambled into helicopters on roofs to flee Vietnam.

In invading Afghanistan, the Red Army achieved complete surprise. Their agents in the Afghan officer corps had made sure that the tanks of the Afghan Army's two armoured divisions had been sent into the workshops and stripped down 'for maintenance'. Anti-tank units were immobilized by an 'inventory' of their weapons. As in Czechoslovakia, the capital's airfield was the Soviet's first target. Spetznaz troops of the 105th Guards Airborne Division swiftly seized Kabul Airport and opened the runways for the unhindered arrival of 280 troop-carrying aircraft which brought in the rest of their division, along with paratroopers of the 103rd and 104th Divisions.

At the same time columns of tanks and AFVs rolled across the northern border with the 357th, 66th, 360th and 201st Motorized Rifle Divisions. Air cover was provided by squadrons of Mig 21 (Fishbed) and Mig 23 (Flogger) fighters. The objectives of these columns were the cities and military bases of Afghanistan and the Salang highway from Kabul to the Soviet border.

In Kabul itself a KGB hit team wearing Afghan Army uniforms attacked the Darulaman Palace, took the guard by surprise and in a running massacre through the corridors of the palace shot down the country's prime minister, Hafizullah Amin, and his family.

The Soviets had made their stooge, Barbrak Karmal, head of state. They were later to claim that the 'Afghan Government' had requested their intervention but that claim does not hold water, because Amin was hardly

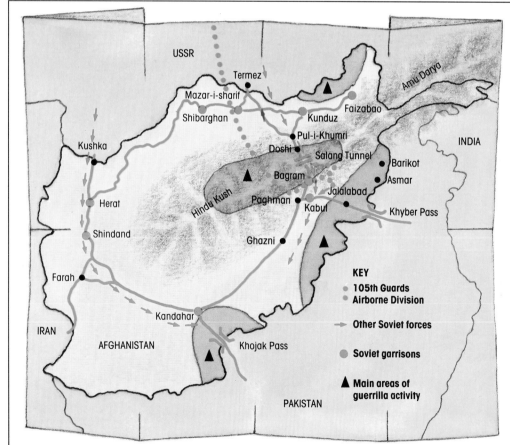

Nine years of fighting has left its scars on Afghanistan. With men like Gearing (above), who fought the guerrilla war in the Panjshir Valley, the Afghan people can set about reconstructing their lives. Changes have already been made in the Soviet establishment, with the recognition of leaders like General Gromov (above right), the last commander of the Soviet forces in Afghanistan, and now importantly placed as Commander of the Kiev military district. The invasion centred on Kabul (left), but in the months that followed, the Mujahideen's hit-and-run raids on convoys (right) plying between the far-flung Soviet garrisons proved devastating to the Soviet forces.

likely to request intervention against himself and Karmal was in Russia when the invasion took place.

In the March 15 1980 edition of *Krasnaya Zvezda*, newspaper of the Soviet Defence Ministry, an editorial entitled Loyalty to the idea of Internationalism, stated: 'Loyal to their internationalist duty, Soviet servicemen, together with the servicemen of other Socialist countries, went to the assistance of fraternal Czechoslovakia in 1968. At the request of Afghanistan's Revolutionary Government a limited contingent of Soviet troops is now fulfilling its internationalist duty on the Democratic Republic of Afghanistan's territory in accordance with the 1978 Treaty of Friendship, Good Neighbourliness and Co-operation between the USSR and the DRA'.

Why then did the Soviet Government set out on this colonialist adventure? Why did they not learn from the disasters that befell the British Army in Afghanistan's wild and inhospitable mountains?

It has been suggested that the invasion was part of a Kremlin plot to expand to the warm waters of the Indian Ocean and to make Pakistan into a vassal state. The truth is that it was a defensive rather than an aggressive move, an attempt by the Soviets to hold on to what they had rather than to acquire more.

Leonid Brezhnev, speaking to the Polish Party Conference on Moscow Radio on November 12 1968, said 'When internal and external forces hostile to Socialism seek to reverse the development of any Socialist country towards a restoration of the Capitalist order . . . this is the concern of all Socialist countries'.

Attempted reform

Afghanistan first came into Russia's orbit after all those years of playing 'the Great Game' in 1971 when Mohammed Daoud, the 'Red Prince', overthrew his cousin, King Zair Shah. But Daoud moved to the right and in April 1978 he too was overthrown and murdered along with 30 of his family. His successor, Nur Taraki, carried out a bloody purge of his opponents and imposed radical agrarian and educational reforms which shocked the fervent Islamic tribesmen. Communism came into direct conflict with Islam and the tribesmen rose in revolt against the unholy atheists.

There then began a period of tension between Taraki and his right-hand man, Hafizullah Amin, which ended in a shoot-out between the two men. Amin packed the Central Committee with his men, ordered Taraki's arrest and had him suffocated with cushions.

While all these mediaeval machinations were taking place the Soviets were following the same path as the Americans in Vietnam. They set up a KGB headquarters in Kabul. They poured in aid and advisers and more and more soldiers. The first Soviets were killed, butchered in an uprising in Herat. And, just as in Vietnam, whole provinces went over to the rebels.

Amin began to look for ways out of the desperate situation in which he was plunged. He started to negotiate with the Mujahideen, made friendly noises to

Above: Red Army tank crews in Afghanistan prepare to be flown home by giant transporter aircraft. The Soviets were defeated by the classic guerrilla tactic, which is to travel light, strike by ambush then disappear into the terrain. Tanks were totally unsuitable for the terrain over which much of the war was fought. Even when the Mujahideen were confronted, they responded with highly portable weapons, such as the Soviet-designed rocket-propelled grenade and launcher (right).

Pakistan and even refused the Soviets control of the Shindad air base near the Iranian border. And in a public rebuff to Russia he demanded the recall of the Soviet ambassador for interfering in the internal affairs of Afghanistan.

It seemed to the Soviets that Afghanistan was slipping out of their grasp. The old fear of encirclement by the West pervaded the Kremlin. *Pravda*, the Communist Party newspaper, later spelt out that fear: 'Our country made no secret of the fact that it would not allow Afghanistan to be turned into a bridgehead for the preparation of imperialist aggression against the Soviet Union'. Brezhnev said that the Soviet Union's hostile frontiers would increase by 1,550 miles (2,500 km) if

Amin stayed in power. The Brezhnev Doctrine of never allowing a Socialist country to stray from the Soviet fold came into play and the Red Army rolled into Kabul.

Flag of revolt

The arrival of the infidels brought out all those warrior-like qualities in the Afghan tribesmen which the British Army had learnt to respect. The green flag of revolt was passed through the hill villages and a holy war declared against the infidels.

At first they were poorly armed with a collector's delight of weapons. Home-made copies of the Lee-Enfield .303, Sten gun, a few prized AK47s stolen or bought from Afghan soldiers, even ancient jezails, muzzle-loaders handed down from father to son, made up the armoury of the Mujahideen, the Holy Warriors.

They fought as their forefathers had fought the British: sniping from the hills with ambushes and sudden rushes down rocky defiles.

Their assets were an unshakeable faith, bravery, an ability to fight in impossible conditions on cruel terrain and an intimate knowledge of that terrain. They lead harsh lives and killing comes easily to them. It is their history, their religion and their way of life which make them such formidable warriors and at the same time are their greatest drawbacks, for they are hopelessly divided on tribal and religious lines.

These divisions are a problem which has persisted throughout their jihad and is even more evident now when the Mujahideen are trying to put a regular army into the field to overthrow the Afghan Government.

Divided into seven main parties, their jealousies and quarrels have spilled over into bloodshed and it is difficult to get them to agree to joint plans of action. The Soviets took advantage of these divisions and with the promise of weapons and gold and land tempted a number of the Afghans to change sides – although many of them promptly changed sides again as soon as they got their reward.

In opposition to these brave, cunning, but often feckless fighters, the Soviet Union fielded an army imbued with a confidence in its fighting ability which derived from its victories in the 'Great Patriotic War' against Nazi Germany.

The wrong war

The Red Army was well-equipped and well-trained and thought itself more than a match for the 'Basmachi' (the bandits), a name originally given to the Central Asians who fought the Red Army in the 1920s. But it was an army trained and equipped for a war against NATO on the plains of northern Europe, an enemy which could be crushed by the sheer weight of shells and tanks and massed regiments. It was neither trained nor equipped to fight small bands of guerrillas.

Its tanks and supply trains were confined to the vulnerable roads where they could be mined and ambushed. One tactic used by the Mujahideen was to dig a deep trench across a narrow road and cover it like an elephant trap. The lead tank would fall in, bringing the convoy to a halt. The guerrillas would then emerge, smear mud over the view slits and pour petrol over the trapped vehicles.

The Red Army found itself fighting the wrong sort of war, a guerrilla war for which its battlefield doctrine had not prepared it and in which its advantages in equipment, firepower and staff work were negated by the difficulties of terrain and the stubbornness of the 'Muj'.

Like Soviet society itself, the army had become smug and resistant to change, run by a generation for whom the Great Patriotic War was the decisive experience in life. Today the army still mirrors Soviet society but both are changing, and the outcome is by no means clear.

Below: BMD light tank of the Soviet airborne forces. Mounted over the 73-mm main gun is a Sagger anti-tank missile.

باغ بالا رستورانت
BAGHE BALA RESTAURA

One of the first lessons of the conflict was that the Red Army had made a great mistake in sending Muslim troops from Central Asia into Afghanistan.

It was an understandable mistake based on logistics. Many of these soldiers were reservists and could be easily transported from states such as Uzbekistan bordering Afghanistan. But they were also of the same stock as certain Afghan tribes and when they arrived they found they were fighting not Basmachi or Chinese and American imperialists – as they had also been told – but deeply religious men who had much more in common with them than the Russians.

The Koran was freely available to them and they began to identify both ethnically and religiously with the men they were supposed to fight. They had to be hurriedly replaced by more dependable troops from other parts of the Soviet Union.

Another problem which became immediately apparent was that the average Soviet conscript was simply not fit enough. Trained to go to war on wheels they were unable to 'yomp' over the Afghan mountains as the Royal Marines did in the Falklands. Combat in the mountains exposed the complacency of officers who attached little importance to the fitness of their men as 'everybody operates in vehicles nowadays'.

Above: The BMD lightweight infantry combat vehicle, used by Soviet airborne troops, spearheaded the rapid and efficient invasion of Afghanistan.

In prolonged operations on foot, signallers who were bowed under the weight of their radio sets and spare batteries – or who lightened their load by ditching spare antennae and batteries – became a major liability in pursuing the guerrillas across difficult terrain.

Like the Americans in Vietnam, they found they needed more and more men to make up for individual inefficiency and loss of morale. In the end, one airborne and five motor rifle divisions along with support units totalling 115,000 men were deployed. There were also sizeable contingents of KGB and GRU agents and special troops.

No armoured divisions took part in the invasion but the infantry and airborne units were supported by a great diversity of standard Soviet armour. Altogether, T-54, T-55, T-62 and T-72 Main Battle Tanks, and probably a few T-80s, saw action. BTR-60/70 amphibious eight-wheeled Armoured Personnel Carriers were extensively used, along with BMP-1/2 and BMD Infantry Fighting Vehicles and BRMD-2 scout cars.

Fire support was provided by the tanks and by self-propelled artillery. The 122-mm 2SI M-1974 and the 155-mm 2S3 M-1973 and 2S5 M-1977 were all used along with 23-mm gun trucks and automatic 30-mm grenade launchers. For a big punch the Red Army's gunners even used Frog-7 battlefield support missiles.

Individual weapons were based on the tried and trusted AK47 family of assault rifles with the usual complement of mortars and rocket-propelled grenades.

Divided allegiance

The Red Army also, in theory, had the support of the Afghan Army. On paper it seemed a formidable force with 80,000 men organized into 14 divisions. Its equipment, which included some ancient T-34 tanks, was second rate compared with the Soviets' kit but should have been sufficiently powerful for it to have seen off the Mujahideen.

The trouble with the Afghan Army was its morale. Most of its soldiers were extremely unwilling and often mutinous conscripts seeking the first opportunity to desert or defect to the rebels, taking their weapons

with them. Some of them were Mujahideen, caught by the press gangs while on surreptitious visits to their families.

The Soviets found them unreliable and most of them were posted to guard duties in cities and fortified posts. Distrust was mutual. The Soviets accused the Afghans of treachery and the Afghans accused the Soviets of interfering with their women and of putting them in indefensible positions. With Soviet soldiers often high on hashish and Afghans hating the infidels, it is not surprising that there were clashes between Afghan units and Soviet troops. Many Soviets argued that there was no point in training and equipping the Afghans because all they were doing was providing trained men and weapons for the Mujahideen.

The degradation of the Afghan Army became noticeable as the war progressed. In 1980-81 there were two Afghan units for every Soviet unit operating against the Mujahideen. By the following year the position had been reversed, with two Soviet units fighting for every Afghan unit of comparable size.

122mm 2S1 Gvozdika

Below: The Soviet Gvozdika 2S1 – a 122-mm self-propelled gun. The hull provides sufficient buoyancy to allow the 2S1 to float with little preparation.

122-mm howitzer fires up to five rounds a minute and has a range of about 9 miles (15 km)

Gunner sights through periscope for indirect fire or through a second sight for direct fire

Commander directs operations to orders and will support only the unit to which the artillery is attached

Loader throws empty shell cases out of his hatch

Air filter at the back of the turret and an overpressure system give capability to operate in NBC environments

Armoured glacis, estimated at 0.6-0.8 inch (14-20 mm) thick, gives protection against only small arms fire and shell fragments

Driver sits to the left of the engine which drives a manual transmission with five forward and one reverse gear

Tracks provide propulsion in water (the SO-122 is fully amphibious) 400-mm wide tracks – replaced by 670-mm wide tracks when operating in snow or in swampy terrain

Variable-height suspension

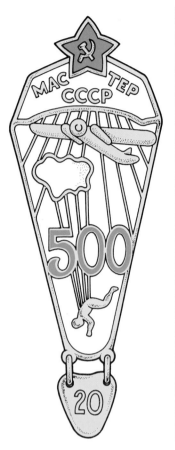

The lion of Panjshir

The aim of the Soviet command was, again as with the Americans in Vietnam, to bring the guerrillas to formal battle where the army's heavy weaponry could be used to full effect. The Soviets chose the strategic Panjshir Valley, north-east of Kabul, as their killing ground.

Opposing them was Commander Ahmed Massoud, the 'lion of Panjshir' who threatened the Bagram airbase and the Salang Highway from his base in the lush valley.

The Soviets and their Afghan allies set out to destroy Massoud and his men in January 1982. The Mujahideen were not prepared for the search-and-destroy operation, although they had been warned by sympathizers in the Afghan Army. They were hit badly by the bitterly cold weather in which they suffered many losses from frostbite, borrowing shoes and clothes from each other to wait in ambush.

Caught on the open plain before the valley proper, and armed only with light weapons, they were forced to fight a defensive battle against infantry supported by armour while under artillery bombardment and air strikes from bombers and helicopter gunships.

For once, fighting on their own terms, the Soviets had victory in their grasp but they were foiled when Afghan Army officers allowed the Mujahideen to slip through the cordon that was tightening around them.

The following year Massoud agreed to a truce with the Soviets, a deal which brought accusations of corruption and treachery against him from his rivals. But he used the respite to arrange alliances with other

Above left: The Soviet airborne insignia. This division has a total strength of about 800 officers and 8,000 men in three airborne regiments and an artillery regiment, plus a number of battalions and companies for support. Above: Afghan troops towards the end of the Soviet involvement in Afghanistan.

field commanders which led to far more effective Mujahideen co-ordination on the battlefield.

In the following year, he returned to the battle and the Soviets launched three major offensives against him in and around Panjshir. By the end of the year, most of the villages had been destroyed by bombing and shellfire and by frustrated Soviet infantry who wantonly killed villagers and set fire to their homes in actions reminiscent of My Lai in Vietnam. Most of the valley's inhabitants who survived fled to Pakistan.

Jammiat-I-Islam, the faction to which Massoud belongs, claimed 'After nine months of war, loss of thousands of men, hundreds of tanks, APCs and trucks and tens of jets and helicopters, at the end of 1984 they did not even have a few families under their control. They were not able to establish a school, a cinema, a clinic or hold a public meeting of the local people for political propaganda.

'All they had achieved was the occupation of some parts of the main valley and defending them by garrisons, out-posts, air raids and minefields. They were bogged down in a hostile environment with no obvious target to attack.'

Battle in the Panjshir Valley

Typical of the type of operation mounted by the Soviets in the Panjshir Valley was an attempt to rescue a number of high-ranking Afghan Government prisoners taken by Massoud when his men captured the defended village of Pushgoor some 31 miles (50 km) inside the valley in June 1985.

The unfortunate prisoners had been inspecting the base when Massoud attacked and their helicopter was shot down. The Mujahideen released the conscript soldiers but kept their officers and the delegation. Then, by means of 'night letters' spread in Kabul, they let the families of the captured men know that they were willing to exchange them for Mujahideen prisoners.

Under pressure from the captured men's families the 'puppet government' in Kabul agreed to negotiate. But the Russians vetoed them and on July 10th started a massive aerial, artillery and rocket bombardment of the Safidcheer area where the prisoners were being held. Antipersonnel mines were scattered by aircraft, helicopters and long-range rockets. These were the classic signs of an impending offensive but the Mujahideen ignored them, lulled by their agreement to negotiate.

It was a mistake which was almost fatal for the Mujahideen. At 4am on July 12th while Massoud, the Ulema (religious council) and a large number of guerrillas were in a side valley of Safidcheer, helicopters

swooped out of the sky to land teams of Spetznaz and airborne commandos all over the area. The Mujahideen and some civilians, 400 people in all, were caught in an area only 3 miles (5 km) square, and were pounded all day by artillery and rockets.

Right: Stalin's organ – the RPU-14 multiple rocket system of World War II fame. The rockets are ballistic and are most effective against mass targets, such as columns of troops. In modern multiple rocket systems, the rockets are independently targetable and guided. Below: A Soviet D30 122-mm howitzer.

During the bombardment, the building in which the prisoners were being kept was hit and most of them were killed or injured. The fighting continued all day. But when darkness fell the Mujahideen and the civilians slipped away across the hills to safety. At dawn the Soviets stormed the valley and found nothing there except the dead and wounded prisoners.

Testing ground

This fierce little battle was notable because the Soviets used it to try out new tactics and weapons. One that particularly disturbed the Mujahideen was a night-seeing device which the Spetznaz used in ambushes and to penetrate the Mujahideen's defensive lines.

They stepped up the weight of their bombs to 2,200

diverted to Afghanistan where they were tested in the field. The Soviets constantly presented the Mujahideen with nasty surprises, including anti-personnel canister bombs filled with needle-sharp flechettes, a fuel-air explosive that kills by a blast of burning gas, a high-angle gun with which AFVs could reach rebels lurking in the steep hills and an automatic 82-mm mortar.

The Red Air Force also introduced some highly effective new aircraft. For close air support they deployed the Su-25 (Frogfoot) which is armed with a 30-mm cannon and can carry bombs, unguided rockets and tactical air-to-surface missiles. It can also loiter over the battlefield for a long time and direct its lethal armament towards the guerilla bases in the hills with great accuracy.

The Soviet Mi-24 Hind helicopter gunship is undisputed king of the battlefield helicopters. Nicknamed the Devil's Chariot by the Mujahideen, the Hind can destroy vehicles and insert troops – two tasks that are often combined. The Hind-A variant (left) has three flight crew, a cabin for eight and a machine gun in the nose. The Hind-D variant (right) has a modified fuselage and a four-barrelled 12.7-mm nose gun. Hinds fell (below) in large numbers to Stinger hand-held missiles.

lb (1000 kg), used a 9.5-inch (245-mm) mortar which fired a shell weighing 290 lb (130 kg) and brought into action a long-range rocket to spread anti-personnel mines. These new weapons were part of the revolution in command, tactics, equipment and training forced on the Red Army by the harsh reality of guerrilla warfare.

In terms of equipment, the ordinary soldiers gave up their long overcoats and were issued with padded combat jackets and, later, with flak jackets. The AK47 was replaced by the AK74. Silenced Tokarev pistols and sub-machine guns were issued to counter-insurgency troops for use in ambushes. Cruel anti-personnel mines in the shape of toys were dropped on villages.

Seismic 'spider-web' mines were developed to lay in the path of rebel parties. They consist of a central command unit linked to six charges each containing nearly 10 lb (4.5 kg) of explosives. Sensors pick up approaching footsteps and, depending on the size of the approaching party, the command unit sets off the appropriate combination of mines. Some weapons and kit destined for issue to the Warsaw Pact forces were

Helicopter gunships

There is no doubt, however, that the Queen of the battlefield was the formidable Mi-24 Hind helicopter gunship which, in various marks, caused much havoc among the Mujahideen. Fast, heavily armoured and carrying a 12.7-mm Gatling gun in a nose turret and rocket pods or bombs on its stub wings, the Hind can also transport a fully armed infantry squad.

It was the Hind which transformed the war in Afghanistan. When the Soviet conscripts first came up against the Mujahideen, they would jump out of their lorries and group around their officer and wait for orders rather than use their initiative to engage the

Mi-24 Hind

Forged titanium hub and high-tensile steel rotor blades can withstand hits from 23-mm cannon

Infra-red suppressors dissipate engine exhaust heat

Air-data probe measures drift, yaw and air speed to aid accurate weapons delivery

Gunner (in front) and pilot sit in separate cockpits with optically flat, bullet-proof windscreens that can withstand hits from 23-mm shells

Rockets most commonly carried are UV-32-57 units, carrying 32 57-mm unguided rockets; AT-6 Spiral anti-tank missiles are mounted on rails at the end of the stub pylons

12.7-mm rapid-fire four-barrelled cannon slaved to under-nose sensors for accuracy

Under-nose sensors include low light-level TV and forward-looking IR (both giving adverse-weather and night capability), and a target detection and ranging radar

Cabin carries reload missiles and up to eight troops fully equipped for insertion into battle

enemy. The revolution in tactics enforced by the nature of the war led to the conscripts being used mainly as garrison and support troops, leaving the task of fighting the Mujahideen to the Spetznaz and other specially trained counter-insurgency troops drawn from airborne and air assault units and carried into battle by helicopter.

On a visit to London on March 10 1986, Mujahideen Commander, Abdul Haq, reported: 'They are using helicopters like tanks, like trucks, like armoured personnel carriers. They attack us with them'.

The Spetznaz, easily identifiable by their blue-and-white striped sailor shirts and red armbands, undertook specialized missions such as the rescue of prisoners and the assassination of Mujahideen leaders. One of their victims was the brilliant guerrilla leader, Abdul Qadir.

The counter-insurgency troops, carried in Hinds, were used to lay ambushes for Mujahideen crossing the mountain paths. They eventually numbered about 20,000, nearly 20 per cent of the Soviet Forces. With their night sights and silenced pistols, they, too, enjoyed considerable success and the Hinds were

Above: Soviet troops practise in mountainous terrain. Experience in Afghanistan showed that troops used to fighting from vehicles were physically unfit.

always there with their massive firepower to protect the commandos if they ran into trouble.

The Mujahideen suffered many casualties from these ambushes and the subsequent attacks from the air. Much of their problem was of their own making for, over-confident, they had begun to group in large formations and were vulnerable to gunship attack.

It was only when they reverted to their traditional guerrilla role that they regained superiority over the Soviets. There were many bloody skirmishes fought at night in rocky defiles and both sides took heavy casualties. It is significant that more than half those soldiers awarded Hero of the Soviet Union medals belonged to airborne units.

The Mujahideen re-equipped as quickly as the Soviets. Help came to them from the USA, Britain, Saudi Arabia, and China. Arms and money were funnelled to them through Pakistan which took its percentage of both but in return allowed the guerrillas to set up their headquarters in the comparative safety of Peshawar – although hit teams of Spetznaz and agents of the WHAD, the Afghan secret service, were active in Kipling's 'City of Evil Countenance'.

The Stinger factor

Copies of Soviet RPGs and recoilless rifles were supplied by China. AK 47s bought with Saudi money came from Egyptian stocks. American aid amounted to some $700 million in 1987 alone. And in 1986 the Americans took the decisive step of supplying the Mujahideen with the Stinger anti-aircraft missile.

After initial difficulties caused by inadequate training, the Stinger deposed the Hind from its throne as ruler of the battlefield. The much feared 'Devil's Chariot' became easy meat for the skilled Stinger marksmen who enjoyed the sort of adulation accorded to Spitfire pilots during the Battle of Britain.

The Hind pilots had to develop dangerous new low-flying tactics, skipping around the mountains, often below the guerrillas. The bombers were forced to fly high and so bomb inaccurately. And all aircraft shot off flares to deceive the Stinger's heat-seeking warhead.

Losses of Hinds and the highly trained commandos they carried became unacceptable. The Mujahideen roamed virtually at will over Afghanistan. Abdul Haq, the guerrilla commander who lost a foot to a mine and has so much shrapnel in his body he sets off the alarms whenever he walks through airport gates, set up camp outside Kabul.

Gorbachev's 'bleeding wound' became a haemorrhage of men, material, money and international prestige. The only way the Soviets could win was to destroy what was left of Afghanistan and take the war into Pakistan, and that was an impossibility. The Red Army had to get out of Afghanistan.

Defeated

They put as good a face on it as possible with the troops being greeted with flowers and kisses when they returned to Soviet soil. But it was all heavily stage-managed. The whole world – especially the Red Army – knew that the soldiers who had rolled into Afghanistan so confidently nine years before had been defeated. According to a young Afghantsi interviewed in a documentary film showing in Moscow: 'How many of my friends died there? And for what?'

What then has the Red Army learnt from this sorry adventure? Besides changes of weaponry, equipment and tactics through lessons learnt the hard way in the field, the Afghan War has had an even deeper effect on the Red Army than lessons that might be expected to be learnt in any war. The British services, for example, are still absorbing the lessons of the Falklands.

What happened in Afghanistan went to the very core of the Soviet military establishment. It has had to rethink its entire concept of command and its use of human resources. It has been a long and hard process, exacerbated by the profound inertia of the Soviet military system. No clearer evidence of this is needed than the length of time it took for the Soviet military press to begin to discuss the lessons of Afghanistan.

It was not until 1982, nearly three years after the invasion, that a few articles dealing with practical problems such as signalling and driving in mountainous terrain began to appear in military journals. They were almost swamped in tales of derring-do about brave Soviet soldiers doing their 'internationalist duty' and they drew their lessons from supposed 'tactical exercises' in Afghanistan.

Right: A Mujahideen lines up a Stinger hand-held heat-seeking missile launcher. The war in Afghanistan was dominated by Soviet troops in their awesome Hind helicopter gunships, until the USA supplied the Mujahideen with Stingers. Initially, the Stingers had limited success, due to technical problems and poor training. Success with Stingers was the chief reason the Soviets had to withdraw from Afghanistan. Below: Soviet RPG-7 anti-tank grenade and launcher provide cover for T54 and T55 MBTs.

It took until 1985 for *Voyenniy Vestnik* (Military Herald) to produce a regular series of articles openly describing combat against the Mujahideen and seeking to prepare young officers for the realities of battle.

Western analysts have been impressed for a long time with the scope and quality of the discussion in Soviet military magazines of the problems of carrying out major military operations in Europe but until very late in the day these same magazines gave no indication of the command and morale problems that officers would face in Afghanistan.

The aftermath

In 1987 the Soviets began to face the facts in public. In May, *Pravda* printed a long critique of the Red Army. It revealed that 12 per cent of all conscripts had to be sent home because they did not meet the required physical standards and it criticized poor training procedures and lack of discipline. It also referred to the fact that many recruits from Central Asia did not know enough Russian to understand orders.

Morale was an even more delicate subject. The extensive bullying of young recruits, the boredom of life in an Afghan outpost, the easy availability of drugs and the temptations of Kabul which even in the midst of the war had more consumer goods on sale than Moscow, are only now beginning to be properly discussed.

The army had to start at the beginning to cope with these problems. Young men are being encouraged to

Above: The Soviet BMP amphibious armoured infantry combat vehicle. Twenty years in service, the outdated 73-mm gun is only now being replaced.

take part in physical training at school to prepare themselves for their call-up. Drastic alterations were also made to the initial training of recruits. Instead of being trained in those units in which they were to spend their two years' service, they were sent to specialized training units where they learnt the basics of mountain warfare before being posted to Afghanistan.

It was then necessary to sort out the next level of command. Combat with the guerrillas demonstrated that the army was woefully short of experienced NCOs, the backbone of any army. Most Soviet NCOs are conscripts themselves, selected before enlistment and with no more experience than the soldiers they lead.

Events in the Afghan War forced Soviet units to operate in small, independent groups. If the officer was knocked out the NCOs had to take command, finding themselves in situations where they not only had to command men in a firefight but also direct artillery and helicopter strikes.

Traditionally, Soviet NCOs have not been expected to learn skills beyond basic map-reading and signalling. Suddenly, they were pitchforked into situations of responsibility for which they were not trained. In February 1989, Colonel General Merimskiy, Head of the Ground Force Combat Training Directorate,

Above: T-54 tanks during manoeuvres. The T-54/55 series has proved to be remarkably durable, and modernization kits for them are on offer. The 100-mm gun is its main weakness. The Soviet T-80 (left) is well-armed with the Kobra gun/missile system. It has a very low silhouette and so presents a small target.

already crowded programme for the average conscript NCO whose skills will in any case be lost at the end of two years' service.

The professional NCO element in the Soviet Army at praposhchik (ensign) rank is not large enough to meet the demands placed on it and is unlikely to become so while army life is regarded by most Soviet citizens as an unpleasant, if necessary, task.

If the Afghan experience illustrated the need for better NCOs, it demonstrated even more clearly the shortcomings of officer training. The military colleges have been attacked for producing young officers who are incapable of taking responsibility without referring to senior officers.

The human factor

There is also great concern about the 'human factor'. The loneliness and brutality of the Afghan War have re-emphasized one of the fundamental lessons of modern warfare: in combat, loyalty to your immediate comrades, the men in your section, is a more powerful motivating force than generalized patriotism or class solidarity.

In trying to encourage such 'small-unit cohesion' the Soviets are using wartime slogans such as: 'Save your comrade, even at the cost of your own life'. However, the achievement of greater comradeship is harder in the Red Army than in most others, principally because of

observed: 'One may have the latest weapons and equipment but if individual soldiers are poorly trained and platoons, companies and battalions are not sufficiently co-ordinated, then one cannot count on success'.

Although it has been easy to see that more training is required, it remains difficult to find the time in an the diversity of the nationalities in the army and the truly horrendous bullying of new recruits.

An average battalion of about 450 men may contain up to 16 different national groupings and as many as seven or eight in a 100-strong company. It is not only the Central Asians who have language problems. Many recruits from the Baltic states either cannnot or will not speak Russian. The result has been that operational units have had to give Russian lessons while in the front.

The first hints of the bully-boy problem came with stories in the military press about 'irregular relationships'. These were at first read in the West as indications of a homosexual problem but Soviet newspapers now talk quite openly about the 'dedovshchina', the tyranny of the 'grandfathers' as the older recruits are known.

Observed Afghantsi Igor Morozov in February 1989: 'We had no idea what it would be like. Before going to Afghanistan I imagined that Soviet soldiers were all on the same side. But our elders made us go through hell. Some behaved like beasts. I can quite understand why some Soviet soldiers defected and started fighting for the other side'.

Great efforts are being made to re-emphasize the role of junior officers in overseeing all aspects of the lives of their men, encouraging them not to 'forget the road to the barrack room door' and to share the hardships of life in the field with their men. They are also being taught to look after the health of their men. Hepatitis significantly weakened the army's strength in Afghanistan.

Officers will only be able to take on this role, however, if they are freed from the processing of the minutiae of military life which is their primary function at the moment. Such tasks are performed in other armies by NCOs but all too often the Soviet officer does the company sergeant-major or section corporal's job rather than anything that a Western army would recognize as an officer's role.

Such shackling to administrative duties and its consequent rigid thinking were poor preparation for commanding men in combat in Afghanistan, and the Red Army is now paying greater attention to developing the basic tactical skills of its junior officer corps.

Below left: The Soviet T-62 main battle tank saw action in Afghanistan. Below: T-62 tanks on exercises in the Soviet Union. The T-62A (right) differs from the T-62 by having a second cupola above the loader.

Soviet T-62

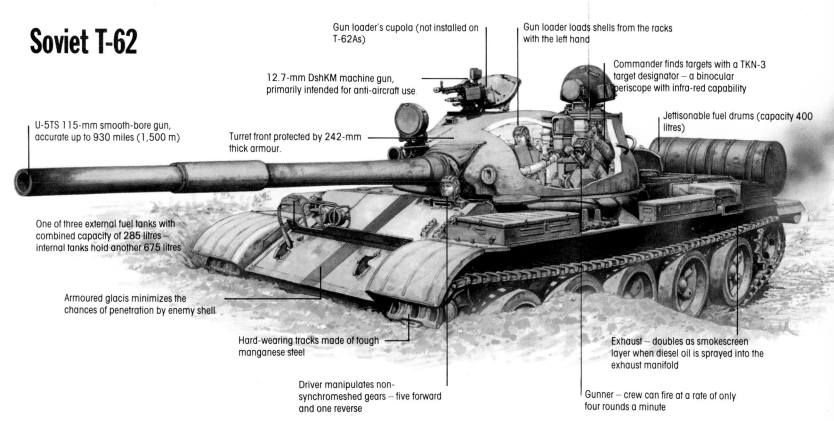

U-5TS 115-mm smooth-bore gun, accurate up to 930 miles (1,500 m)

Turret front protected by 242-mm thick armour.

12.7-mm DshKM machine gun, primarily intended for anti-aircraft use.

Gun loader's cupola (not installed on T-62As)

Gun loader loads shells from the racks with the left hand

Commander finds targets with a TKN-3 target designator – a binocular periscope with infra-red capability

Jettisonable fuel drums (capacity 400 litres)

One of three external fuel tanks with combined capacity of 285 litres – internal tanks hold another 675 litres

Armoured glacis minimizes the chances of penetration by enemy shell

Hard-wearing tracks made of tough manganese steel

Driver manipulates non-synchromeshed gears – five forward and one reverse

Exhaust – doubles as smokescreen layer when diesel oil is sprayed into the exhaust manifold

Gunner – crew can fire at a rate of only four rounds a minute

Such abilities as a good eye for terrain, the co-ordination of a range of weapons and arms of service, and possession of a detailed knowledge of the enemy became literally matters of life or death. Old military lessons such as marksmanship, driving across rugged country, the value of reconnaissance and straight-forward field discipline (like not allowing the troops to drink all their water at once) had to be relearnt.

Lessons unlearned

From the writings of some senior officers, such as the current Defence Minister, Colonel General Dmitry Yazov, the army is aware of its shortcomings in the tactical handling of troops. But will the lessons remain learnt or will the Red Army, relieved of the embarrass-ment of Afghanistan, retreat into bureaucratic inertia just as the US Army turned its back on the lessons of Vietnam?

Alexander Karpienko, a mine-scarred poet watching the Soviet retreat across the Oxus in February 1989 had this to say: 'It was a mistake, a very big mistake, but we can learn from our mistakes. The war in Afghanistan has made us wiser, allowed us to think more clearly about ourselves and about our country'.

Afghanistan showed that major changes such as the granting of greater authority in tactical decision-making and the encouragement of initiative in junior officers were essential. But will they be carried out, implying as they do the need for similar changes in Soviet society as a whole? Will perestroika rule in the Red Army?

The men most likely to force these changes through belong to the 'Afghan Brotherhood', the young generals who served in the war and have now been appointed to

Life as a Soviet recruit

Traditionally, when a young man was called up to join the Tsar's army, his departure was celebrated as a wake, for his family feared that they would never hear from him or see him again. That attitude lingers today. Compulsory service in the 5,000,000-strong Red Army is universally hated.

Training starts at school where pupils are taught drill and weapons training and are lectured on the glories of the Red Army. Conscripts are registered at 17 and called up a year later. Each year, in spring and autumn, round-ups of 1.3 million young men are taken into the Red Army.

Not everybody goes. Students, largely as the result of the Afghanistan experience, are no longer called up. Families with influence make sure their sons stay at home. And many young men simply go on the run, risking three years in the labour camps.

Those sucked into the system start their two years service as 'greenies' at a recruit centre. They arrive with hangovers from their own wake and in old clothes, fearful that good clothes will be stolen. Their first experience of army life is to have their head shaven. Many of them, even those carrying school certificates of Readiness for Labour and Defence, are in poor physical condition and, unable to cope with army life, are sent home.

The remainder start a harsh regime of training not unlike recruit training in most armies but with far fewer amenities and comforts.

Food is plentiful but boring. 'Kasha' – buckwheat porridge – is a staple of the recruit's diet. He gets herrings, occasionally pork or mutton, thick soup, bread, and fruit compote but very little fresh salad or vegetables. Cheese and eggs are rarely served. Everything is eaten with a spoon.

On this diet recruits undergo a harsh routine of physical training and intensely boring political indoctrination. There is a 2-mile (3.2-km) run before breakfast then drill, assault course, drill, weapons training and drill. Lectures and kit cleaning occupy the evenings. There might just be time to watch television. Any old soldier would know the routine.

Compared with Western or even other Soviet Bloc recruits, however, the greenies live in spartan conditions. They sleep in bunks in overcrowded barrack huts. There are none of the amenities built into modern Western barracks. There is no constant hot water. The Soviet recruit gets a steam bath once a week and personal hygiene is a bleak affair. A strip of white cloth is sewn on to his uniform collar to show his officer if he has washed his neck.

He gets paid £7 a month and there is little that he can do with that. Not that he has much chance to spend it. He is not allowed out of barracks until he is fully trained and even then passes are hard to win. Officially, a Soviet conscript is allowed ten days home leave during his two years service but unless he is serving near his home travel difficulties make it worthless.

Facilities for entertainment are as spartan as the barracks. Sometimes the recruits are entertained by groups of singers and dancers but as they work from six in the morning until ten at night, with the evenings spent in the 'Lenin Rooms' where they receive political indoctrination, there is little time for relaxation.

Soviet troops during a training session with a Hind helicopter. Deficiencies in procedures and in combat readiness were revealed in Afghanistan. Until these were remedied, Spetznaz troops, the elite of Soviet forces, were relied on to seek out the Mujahideen.

senior positions. They form a tight-knit clique within the army and have been given responsibility at an early age in an army of old generals. There are brigade commanders as young as 34 and some men in their late 30s are commanding divisions. It is they who can bring pressure to bear for the reform of the military doctrine which has persisted since the defeat of Nazi Germany.

Extensive changes have already been made to the command and communications systems because of the introduction of new technology. But it will be up to men such as Lieutenant General Boris Gromov, last commander of the Soviet forces in Afghanistan, and now importantly placed as commander of the Kiev military district, to ram home the lessons of that conflict.

Another influentially placed member of the Afghan Brotherhood is General Salamanov, who trained the Afghan Army for two years and is now head of the General Staff Academy in Moscow.

The old guard will fight a bitter rearguard action against the Brotherhood's reforms, arguing that Afghanistan was a side show and that the old values would prevail in any general European conflict. They point out that the Wehrmacht won many tactical victories in the final years of World War II but the Russians won all the operational victories.

However, their time may be coming to an end. The Brotherhood officers have already rewritten the book of tactics to take account of their Afghan experiences and, more importantly, President Gorbachev is clearing out the old deadwood in his slashing cutback of the Soviet Forces.

Meanwhile, other problems loom. Soviet students have listened to the tales of drug-taking and bullying and death from Afghanistan and there is a groundswell of opposition to conscription.

The army will argue that its commitments are so large it could not fulfill them with a volunteer army. But with a smaller, professional army with a proper corps of NCOs and efficiently trained officers led by the Afghan Brotherhood, the Red Army could absorb the lessons of that conflict and be a much more formidable force than it is today.

When General Gromov walked out of Afghanistan across the bridge over the Oxus he said: 'I didn't look back'. But he will time and again and so will the whole of the Red Army.

Below: Soviet troops withdraw from Afghanistan. In a phased withdrawal, motorized rifle units stationed outside Jalalabad left in columns for the border.

The veterans come home

'Our wars were different, but our stories, they are the same.' said Igor Yepufanov, a 23 year-old student from Moscow University. 'I have friends I have never spoken to like this. But these guys, they are like my brothers. They know.'

Igor is an 'Afghantsi', a veteran of the war in Afghanistan and the guys he was talking about were a group of American veterans from Vietnam who had flown to Moscow to help the Afghantsi come to terms with the physical and mental traumas of a vicious guerrilla war.

There are indeed great similarities in the experiences of the unwilling conscripts who fought the wars in Afghanistan and Vietnam, not least the impact of their war's brutality on individuals. No atrocity of the horror of My Lai has yet come to light in Afghanistan but that may be because Soviet reporters do not have the same freedom as American war correspondents. Certainly, there have been many examples of well-authenticated acts of careless murder by the Soviets.

Like the Americans, the Soviets sought to wipe out the pain of the war in drugs and alcohol but as booze was expensive they turned more to the cheap, easily available, hashish and opium of the Afghan hills.

Alexander Kalandarishvili who invited the American veterans to his home in Moscow said: 'Everyone of us there tried drugs. Every other one was an occasional user and every tenth was a regular user.'

Disillusionment with the government and the people in the 'real world' at home are common themes. But Soviet casualties were not even given the honour of a military funeral. If they left Afghanistan on the 'Black Tulip', the name they gave the aircraft which flew the coffins home, they were forgotten as well as dead.

Local authorities refused to print death notices or allow headstones which carried the forbidden word: Afghanistan. Facilities for the wounded were as bad as those for the dead. Amputees faced great difficulties in getting proper treatment and being fitted with artificial limbs. For a long time, the very mention of casualties was barred from the Soviet media.

There was little help for the Afghantsi in resettling into civilian life. Many, having experienced the need for real discipline in the field, are shocked by the corruption and inefficiency they find at home. Some have formed

Below: Soviet troops return from Afghanistan in good spirits. For many of them, it is the beginning of a long period of readjustment to life at home and trying to forget the terrible experiences of the war.

The Soviet Army returns home – to Uzbekistan (above) and Termez (below) – at the end of a war that threatened to drain the resources of their country.

vigilante groups and beat up punks and crooks; others have dropped out.

The families of the Afghantsi are well aware of what has happened to them but Russia as a nation has not suffered the great soul-searching of the USA over Vietnam. This is because, while it is being admitted the war was a mistake, very close control was kept over the reporting of the war and the ordinary Russian still thinks that the Red Army went to Afghanistan to do its 'internationalist duty'.

The Soviets learnt the Vietnam lesson: the retreat across the Oxus was feted as a victory, quite unlike the American flight from the roof of the Saigon embassy. Nevertheless, the experiences of some 200,000 Afghantsi has bitten deep into their souls. It is said of them that 'they seem to be looking at some far away place'.

Afghanistan is also being dealt with seriously in films and books. In one starkly shot documentary film called 'Return' one veteran says: 'I was in a surgical ward. I saw healthy boys without legs, without arms. The war has turned our boys into cripples, and what's more it has left our society crippled. People who return from that war are moral cripples'.

Another Afghantsi in the film says: 'I feel I want to smash everything. In Afghanistan, everything seemed easy, everything was clear. Here, nothing is clear'.

Even the influential *Literaturnaya Gazeta* has at last broached the subject of the 'moral deformation' inflicted on the soldiers by the war. Truly an echo of Vietnam.

Chapter 5
SEA WAR:
Fast
Patrol Boats

Known variously as Patrol Boats, Fast Attack Craft and Rocket Cutters, the Fast Patrol Boat is a prized possession in the fleets of the world's navies. Its high speed, small size and large arsenal give it the image of an agile predator able to command a vast range with a shark-like lethality. The crews number a mere handful and the vessels are usually commanded by junior officers. Cheap at the price, and inexpensive to run and man, this type of craft is favoured by the navies of rich and poor nations alike. In every sense, it is the David to the Goliath warships.

Left: The design of this SNV DHOA fast missile attack craft of the Oman Navy is based on an enlargement of the 220-tons full load 144-ft *Tenacity* built by Vosper Thornycroft (1967-69). It has a deepened hull forwards, giving two decks and greater seaworthiness.

The size of vessel that passes for a Fast Patrol Boat (FPB) varies greatly – typical displacements range between 15 and 600 tons. Similarly, the size and speed of FPBs reflect the armament they carry, which varies from machine guns to missiles. Even the name is not universally agreed. The US Navy use the prefix P (for Patrol), followed by other designations, and the USSR calls its Osa- and Komar-sized boats Rocket Cutters. Over the years, the Royal Navy has used various descriptions, settling on Fast Patrol Boat in 1950, but these craft are also called simply Patrol Boat (PB) and Fast Attack Craft, armed with either guns – FAC(G) – or missiles – FAC(M).

Various hull designs have been tried. Most early types were stepped-hull, planing boats – later examples being the Soviet P.4 and East German Libelles. These were fast in calm water, but difficult to handle in high waves. Hard-chine hulls – as used, for example, in most British boats from the 1930s-60s – were easier to handle than planing boats but less seaworthy than the slower, round-bilge type. Modern hydrodynamics however have evened out many of the differences in handling between these traditional hull-forms, so performance depends largely on the person at the helm. Vosper's designer, Peter Du Cane, demonstrated the British hard-chine *Brave Borderer* at full speed (50 knots) in a Force 6 wind, but he was exceptionally skilled, and nothing like that performance could be safely achieved in service.

Other designs include hovercraft, surface-effect vessels and hydrofoils – both the basic fixed type and the fully submerged computer-controlled foils used on boats like the USN's *Pegasus*. None of these designs are new. For example, the Austro-Hungarian Navy tried a surface-effect FPB during World War I. Perhaps stranger than any was the Italian Grillos (also from World War I) designed with caterpillar tracks to climb over the harbour defence boom at Pola.

Whatever designs are available, navies get only what they can afford, and a notable attempt has been made in the late 1980s by the Danes to economize by using modular systems to unify the functions of FPB, patrol and minesweeping in one type – the Stanflex 300. To change function, they simply change the modules.

Flying the flag

Some navies acquire FPBs simply for prestige. Usually, however, FPBs are used for defence. They are intended to protect the coastal waters from the enemy, which might be a single saboteur or the largest warships. Most FPBs can also be used offensively – for example, to infiltrate saboteurs or to attack convoys, as in the Gulf War.

Each country's needs for FPBs are different, and within each navy, the role of its FPBs may change with circumstances. In the Israeli Navy, for example, FPBs were at first minor assistants to larger warships. Later, especially after the sinking of the *Eilat*, they became the mainstay of the navy. As the navy's role gradually became more important, and as technology – particularly Over-The-Horizon (OTH) missiles – improved, the size of the FPBs increased through the Sa'ars and Reshefs to the helicopter-carrying Aliyahs and their Romat half-sisters. The basic type has now evolved into 1,150-ton corvettes to be built in the USA to the Israeli design. In addition, there has always been the small Dabur type, to guard the coast against terrorists.

The adoption of the 200-mile (322-km) Economic Exclusion Zone (EEZ) has forced a reappraisal of the size of boat required for all navies, although in general FPBs are not ideal for policing this zone. What is mostly needed is a slower, more seaworthy ship. Often, FPBs are used because they are available, not necessarily because they are the most suitable craft. Besides, preparations for war, or even a limited war such as Vietnam, require different craft from policing the peace.

Some navies need FPBs only to train the crew of larger warships. The Royal Navy used FPBs for this purpose from the late 1950s until an economy review caused the section to be disbanded in 1980. The navy even built the three unarmed Scimitar-class vessels, developed from the Brave design, specially for training. Perhaps the strangest vessel built for training (and trials) is the Finnish *Isku*. Above the deck, this resembles an Osa, with its four Styx SSMs (Surface to Surface Missiles). It has a standard landing-craft hull, although fitted with more powerful engines.

The right weapon

The first recognisable ancestors of the modern FPB appeared in the later part of the 19th century. There had always been a need for a vessel small enough to be built in larger numbers, but powerful enough to destroy large ships. The breakthrough came with the series production of a suitable weapon – the Whitehead torpedo – and the introduction of lightweight triple-expansion steam engines. By 1900, almost all navies had at least a few torpedo boats, and some – for

Left: A painting of the Royal Navy's *HMS Brave Borderer* (P1011) torpedo gunboat at speed. Built by Vosper Thornycroft and launched on January 7 1958, it was an example of the final flowering of the traditional FPB. Developments in weapons and sensors demanded a larger, longer-ranged hull.
Below: The US Navy's *USS Hercules* (PHM-2) Pegasus class patrol hydrofoil powered by gas turbines.

example, the French – had them in large numbers.

The steam engines were soon superseded by internal-combustion engines, and World War I set the guidelines for subsequent developments. The major European powers built fast attack craft and slower, gun-armed patrol boats (the Allies making use of commercial designs produced in the United States). There were many pointers to the future.

Under the right conditions, these vessels sank even the largest ships – for example, in 1918, Italian Motoscafo Anti-Sommergible (MAS) or Anti-Submarine Motorboats sank the Austro-Hungarian battleship *Svent Istvan*. They proved invaluable for patrol work, for mine-laying, and for special duties. The British even made successful trials with remote control from the air. Equally importantly, these early PBs demonstrated the limitations – the restricted range,

poor seaworthiness and vulnerability to attack from the air, as when a flotilla of British Coastal Motor Boats (CMBs) was caught and destroyed by German aircraft.

The most successful designs were the British Thornycroft-built CMBs and the Italian MAS boats. The stepped, planing hull CMBs were built in three sizes – 40 ft (12.2 m), 55 ft (16.8 m) and 70 ft (21.3 m). The two smaller types launched forward-facing torpedoes backwards over the stern, then swerved out of the way as the torpedoes picked up speed.

The 70-ft boats were mine-layers. Their greatest moment came immediately after World War I when a small force under Lt-Cdr Agar penetrated the Soviet Baltic Fleet's base at Kronstadt and sank a battleship and a cruiser. Thornycroft sold a number abroad between the wars, and most Soviet and Japanese World War II torpedo boats were derived from the Thornycroft design. The last type that owes something to this concept – the East German Libelle class – is only just being taken out of service.

The MAS boats' greatest virtue was their lightweight reliable petrol engines, particularly those made by Isotta Frashini. The Italians continued to develop their boats and engines in the 1920s and 1930s, unlike the British. So long as the French side of the English Channel was not in hostile hands, the Royal Navy had little need for FPBs except in places such as Hong Kong. When Germany began to re-arm, Hubert Scott-Paine revived British torpedo boat development with

Below: The three Royal Navy Scimitar-class fast vessels built specifically for training. From top to bottom are *HMS Cutlass, HMS Scimitar* and *HMS Sabre*.

hard-chine hulled boats made by his British Power Boat Company in the early 1930s. And when his main rival Vosper produced the standard British 70-ft (21.3-m) Motor Torpedo Boat (MTB) using Isotta Fraschini engines, Scott-Paine's design became the basis of most subsequent US PT-Boats (Patrol Torpedo Boats).

Meanwhile Lurssen, in collaboration with the German Navy, was designing the S-Boote (Schnelleboote – Fast Boats). With a few early exceptions, all were round-chine hulled and powered by high-speed diesels (mainly from Daimler-Benz). Slower than the British and Italian boats, they were larger, better armed, and generally more robust.

So far as FPBs were concerned, World War II was in many ways a replay of World War I, but on a larger scale. Certain areas proved suitable for FPB operation – the Baltic, English Channel and southern North Sea, Mediterranean and south-eastern Pacific. The same is true today, with the addition of the northern Indian Ocean, the Gulf and the Caribbean.

When Italy entered the war in 1940, the British were cut off from supplies of suitable lightweight, powerful and reliable engines, for which the US Packard (not the licence-built Merlin, although a few of these were used) was a poor substitute. Another problem was that until suitable weapons appeared late in the war, the 70-ft MTB was too small to carry guns capable of defeating the larger and better armed S-boote.

As a temporary measure, separate gun-armed escorts – Motor Gun Boats (MGBs) – were produced out of experimental, high-speed Motor Anti/Submarine Boats (MA/SBs), and nine elaborate 260-ton (full load) 146-ft (44.5-m) steam gun boats were built. By the end of the war, the small MTBs were much better armed and, with the dual-purpose Fairmile D type, size had crept up to that of other navies.

The Italians, who found MAS boats too small, went to larger Lurssen-type S-boote. The German Navy was generally satisfied with its choice, although armament increased and they would have liked more speed. The USN stuck with its 80-ft (24.4-m) PT-boats throughout the war, but by 1945 they were overloaded with radar, Electronic Countermeasures (ECM) and extra guns.

The first post-war decade saw the construction of stop-gap boats to replace wartime MTB, PT, Soviet and S-boote designs, followed by improved construction techniques and the replacement of petrol engines by diesels. Examples of these are the British Korean War Gay and Dark classes. At the same time, trials with gas turbines in a number of countries led to the final flowering of the traditional FPB, exemplified by the superb 50-kt 99-ft (30.2-m) British Brave class and its derivatives, powered by Proteus gas turbines. Built by Vosper in the late 1950s and early 1960s, they were rapidly overtaken by developments in weapons, sensors and functions which demanded a much larger, longer-ranged and, if necessary, slower hull to accommodate the improved sophistication.

PT-109

John F Kennedy as an Officer in the Pacific during World War II where he experienced his boat being cut in two.

On the night of August 1 1943 an action took place that has gone down in American naval and political history. Lt (later President) John F Kennedy USNR was in command of PT-109, an 80-ft (24.4-m) Elco-built PT Boat, with a crew of 12 other officers and men. Their main weapons were 21-inch (533-mm) torpedoes and a 37-mm gun.

PT-109 was one of the 15 boats from MTB Flotilla I that were serviceable after a Japanese air attack on the base at Rendova Harbour on Lumbari Island – one of the Solomon Island chain in the southwest Pacific. It sailed with the others to intercept four Japanese destroyers trying to reach the Japanese base on the southern point of Kolombangara Island – the 'Tokyo Express' – so called because of the regularity with which Japanese destroyers had sailed to re-supply their garrisons since the American invasion of Guadalcanal a year before.

Many of the PT Boats had recently arrived, and there had been little time to practice tactics. It is therefore not surprising that they had a total lack of success in the confused night action that ensued. Kennedy manoeuvred PT-109 to try to torpedo the larger destroyer *Amagiri*. Instead, *Amagiri* – probably accidently – cut PT-109 in two. Two of the crew were never seen again, and some of the others were badly burned in the fire from the petrol. The 2,090-ton *Amagiri* steamed on, to be sunk by a mine in the Makassar Straits on April 23 1944.

Kennedy gathered the survivors together, and – towing the worst-burned one himself – made them swim to the nearest island. They survived on what they could find, with Kennedy (and when he was too exhausted, Ensign Ross) swimming out each night to try to contact a PT Boat patrol. Moving from island to island, on the fourth day they met some Melanesian natives who took messages to an Australian Coast Watcher – one of the intelligence officers organized by the RAN. On the sixth night they were rescued by PT Boats, but President Kennedy was left with a legacy of back problems for the rest of his life.

Action

The most influential single action was the sinking of the Israeli destroyer *Eilat* 14.5 miles (7.2 km) off the Egyptian coast on October 21 1967. Besides changing the Israeli Navy almost overnight into an all-FPB and submarine force, the three Styx fired by Egyptian Komars from their own harbour forced Western navies to accept the SSM revolution started by the USSR.

Styx also performed well in the Indo-Pakistani War of 1971, when Indian Osas used the SSM to sink the Pakistani Destroyer *Khaibar* and minesweeper *Muhafiz* off Karachi, as well as several merchant ships. The same war underlined the FPB's vulnerability to air attack. On December 4 1971, in various locations, all four Pakistani Town-class patrol boats were attacked by Indian Air Force and Navy jets. Three were sunk (one was later salvaged by Bangladesh) and one was severely damaged.

In the October 1973 Arab-Israeli War, the Arab Styx was out-classed by the Israeli Gabriel. Although training and superior Electronic Warfare (EW) equipment influenced the result, Styx's limitations helped the Israeli boats to evade all the 90 or so incoming missiles fired by the Syrian and Egyptian FPBs. In reply, Gabriel-equipped FPBs sank six Syrian boats (and several merchant ships) in three nights off Latakia and Dametia (two with the aid of gunfire because of Gabriel's small warhead), and between three and five Egyptian boats over several days.

Although the Israelis have seen no major FPB actions since, their current mix of Harpoon and Gabriel SSMs with several different guidance systems on a variety of long-ranged FPBs makes them a formidable force. Harpoon is a capable weapon, and the 12 supplied to Iran before the overthrow of the Shah have since been used to good effect. Some have been used from Iranian Kaman-class Combattante II boats against Iraqi FPBs in the Gulf War, and the threat posed by them played a part in the action on July 3 1988 when the *USS Vincennes* shot down the Iranian Airbus.

Some minor actions have been extremely important politically. The attack by three North Vietnamese P.4 torpedo boats on the USN destroyer *Maddox* on August 2 1964, after it and its sister *Turner Joy* had been coat-trailing off the North Vietnamese coast, formed the basis of the Gulf of Tonkin Resolution that consolidated US involvement in Vietnam. Similarly, the attack by three Israeli boats and aircraft on the USN intelligence ship *Liberty* in June 1967, and the capture of the USN intelligence ship *Pueblo* by North Korean gunboats in January 1968 were more important politically than militarily.

The *Maddox* action and the confusion that night over whether another attack was underway, as well as the *Vincennes* action, clearly show the advantages that small, fast well-armed craft can have even when facing well-equipped and trained heavier forces. They are difficult to detect, and can be difficult to destroy.

Survivability

Surprisingly few FPBs are destroyed in combat, and some last well over 30 years in service. There have naturally been a number lost in accidents, some of which have been bizarre. Two, for example, were lost overboard in separate accidents while returning from being fitted with advanced equipment in the UK. The Omani *Al Bushra* was swept overboard in a gale in the Bay of Biscay in November 1978 and was never recovered. The Egyptian 6 October-class No 791 was more fortunate in that after falling overboard on December 16 1980 it was salvaged, refitted, and returned to service nearly two years later. The Bahamas had an FPB sunk by mistake by a Cuban MiG-21 – Cuba later paying $0.5 million compensation. Turkey lost the Kartal-class *Melten* on September 25 1985 when it was cut in two by the Soviet training ship *Khasan*, and also lost an Asheville-class through internal explosions. Algeria lost an Osa and had two more badly damaged when a Styx SSM exploded by accident.

Other ways in which FPBs have been lost include attempted coups, such as the one in South Yemen in January 1986 that resulted in at least two Osas being destroyed. Sometimes FPBs survive when least expected. For example, when Turkey invaded Cyprus in July 1974 most of Cyprus's six P.4 boats were sunk trying to attack the landings. One was beached and captured, and it is now preserved in Turkey.

On three occasions, the French have temporarily embargoed the delivery of FPBs they have built – Israeli Sa'ars in 1967, Iranian Kamans in 1979, and Libyan Bier Grassas in 1981. In the two former cases,

Left: SS-N-2 Styx missiles on their launchers on a Komar-class missile patrol boat. SS-N-2 was the first FPB SSM in service and is still the most widely used.

the aftermath was odd. The five Israeli Sa'ars escaped from Cherbourg (with the connivance of senior French officials) in 1969, thinly disguised as the Norwegian oilfield supply boats *Starboat 1-V*; on the delivery voyage of the three Iranian Kamans after the embargo was lifted in August 1981, *Tabarzin* was seized by Iranian Royalists and temporarily returned to Toulon.

Limitations

FPBs will always be small, flimsy vessels with limited electronics and armament – they are not true deep-water craft. Any attempt at improving them results in them being over-large and expensive. It is impossible to reconcile the conflicting factors of size, cost, speed and striking power. There must always be compromises. For example, twice as many MM40 Exocet SSMs can be carried for the same weight of MM 38s, but at extra cost and with increased volume and weight for improved fire-control to get the best out of the missile.

Speed is always expensive. Two 20-knot boats can be built for about the same price as one similarly sized 30-knotter, but there are other penalties. Although the

Below: Kaman-class missile fast attack craft, *Peykan* (P224), of the Iranian Navy. The Iranians have made extensive use of such vessels in the war with Iraq.

Australian and New Zealand Fremantle and Lake classes are slow and robust for FPBs, they proved too fragile for areas like the Bass Strait. A larger, slower, more robust vessel (like the Osprey 55 used by the Burmese, Danish, Moroccan, Senegalese and Greek Navies) may be a better choice for policing a 200-mile EEZ than an FPB. The British found the same with the hydrofoil Speedy.

Small size has always been the FPB's main defence against larger ships, but it limits the amount of defensive armament and EW equipment that can be carried. Larger hulls with greater capacity are much bigger targets, and are more expensive. Even the largest may have inadequate defences. The Libyan 675-ton Nanuchka *Tariq Ibn Ziyad* was just as easy for the USN to sink as the 311-ton Combattante II *Waheed* in the actions in the Gulf of Sidra in March 1986.

Builders

Three countries predominate in the building of FPBs: the USSR and China by sheer numbers, and West Germany by the omnipresence of the Lurssenwerft in the design of modern Western FPBs, as well as by the numbers it has constructed in its own yards. Other important countries are Britain, France, Israel, North and South Korea, Scandinavia and the USA. Australia and Yugoslavia build FPBs for export.

In Britain, Vosper Thornycroft (VT, who merged in 1966) have been building torpedo boats and FPBs since the mid-1930s (Vosper) and late 19th century (Thornycroft) respectively. Thornycroft, with their CMBs,

were the first firm to achieve major success with fast petrol-engined torpedo boats. Vosper, under Peter Du Cane, produced the classic early World War II MTB, and in the 1950s and early 60s the equally classic Brave gas turbine type.

Like Thornycroft, the Lurssen yard at Vegesack in Germany started in the late 19th century. They turned to FPBs in World War I, and between the wars they produced the standard S-boote design – the basis of all their subsequent boats. After a post-war interval, they were allowed to return to full-time FPB design and construction. Building from the S-boote, they produced the Jaguar class and its derivatives for the West German and other navies, the Spica type (in collaboration with the Swedish Navy) for Sweden, and the Combattante type for CMN in France.

Their 118-ft, 147-ft, 187-ft and 203-ft (36-m, 45-m, 57-m and 62-m) types are the world standard, variants being built in France, Indonesia, Israel, Malaysia, Singapore, South Africa, and Spain, as well as West Germany. The largest boats are mainly used as leaders

for the 147-ft type – as with the West German 187-ft Type 143 and 143A, the Kuwaiti 187-ft and the Bahraini and United Arab Emirate 203-ft boats. The Bahraini 203-ft boats carry helicopters for OTH targeting and mid-course guidance, as do the 203-ft Israeli Aliyahs.

In the West, the other three main independent FPB designers are the French, Italian and US yards. In France, while CMN has concentrated on the Lurssen Combattante types, and the Patras and Super Patras, built mainly for the French Navy, SFCN has produced the less well-armed and more seaworthy P.48 156-ft (47.5-m) and PR72 187-210-ft (57-64-m) types, and CNE has concentrated on 92-105-ft (28-32-m) types.

During the past decade, CNR in Italy has built large boats for Libya, Ecuador and Iraq, the Ecuadorian six having a helicopter platform, and two of the Iraqi six having a platform and a hangar. Breda has sold a number of boats, and Fincantieri has built the large, seaworthy private venture Saetta.

US interest in building FPBs has depended on the current military preoccupation. The Cuban crisis

Left: Britain's *HMS Speedy* (P296), a Vosper Thornycroft hydrofoil used to police Britain's 200-mile Economic Exclusion Zone.

accelerated the submerged hydrofoil programme. The Grumman Flagstaff formed the basis of three hydrofoils built for Israel in the early 1980s, and the Boeing Tucumcari tested the technology for the USN's Pegasus PHMs (Patrol Hydrofoil Missile), the reduced Italian Sparvieros, the abortive British Speedy and the Indonesian fast troop transports. Vietnam designed and built the Ashvilles and Swifts. The 164-ft (50-m) Asheville design was taken up by South Korea, and then built in modified form by Taiwan and Indonesia as well. The only other major modern US FPBs are the nine Al Sidiq class built for Saudi Arabia at the start of the 1980s.

In terms of numbers and new developments, the USSR has easily outbuilt anyone else. The first major classes were the P.4 and P.6 torpedo boats, followed by the Komars – a P.6 derivative, and the first SSM-armed FPB. The first purpose-built SSM-armed FPB was the 126-ft (38.4-m) Osa. After 30 years, it is still the most numerous class of SSM-armed FPB in service. In place of the Komars' two Styx SSMs, the Osas have four tubes – the front ones angled at 12 degrees to the horizontal, and the rear at 15 degrees to allow the SSMs to be fired over the front ones.

The Osa hull formed the basis of a whole family of FPBs – the shortened Stenka torpedo boats, the surface-piercing fixed hydrofoil Turyas (using technology developed from the smaller Pchelas, themselves based on the civilian Strelas) and Matkyas and the export MOLs. There have been a large number of one-off and small-build classes of hydrofoils – alongside moderate numbers of the 198-ft (60.3-m) surface displacement Nanuchkas and the succeeding 185-ft (56.5-m) Tarantuls.

Chinese designs have mainly followed those of Soviet FPBs. Besides direct copies, such as the Huang Feng Osa 1 type, and the indigenous Shanghai- and Hainan-class patrol boats, most Chinese FPBs are developments of Soviet types. Some have been steel-hulled variants of the P.6 type, including the Shantung-class – the first major series-production naval hydrofoil. North Korea has followed the pattern set by China.

A profitable sideline for a number of Western yards has been the refitting or completing of smaller navies' FPBs. Examples are the re-engining and refitting of Libyan FPBs by Italy, and the outfitting of the Komar-based Egyptian 6 October class in Britain.

Machinery

Since World War II, lightweight high-speed diesels have completely replaced petrol (gasoline) engines in FPBs, and more than three-quarters of all FPB diesels in all non-communist countries are made by the West German firm, MTU, and their Mercedes-Benz predecessors. Most are the 16-cylinder 16V538 and 16V956 types, developing about 4,000-4,900 hp (3,000-3,700 kW). Most of the others are powered by diesels built by American General Motors and Caterpillar, British Paxman (Valentia and Ventura) and French AGO and SEMT-Pielstick. Few Western boats are powered by gas turbines, except hydrofoils, in which weight considerations are all-important. The standard Western FPB gas turbine is the General Electric LM-2500, rated at up to about 25,000 hp (18,750 kW). A number of earlier FPBs used the British Proteus, as does the Italian

Below: The West German Type 143 Schnellboote. This standard design was produced between the World Wars by the Lurssen yard at Vegesack and has been the basis of all FPBs subsequently produced by them.

German Navy Type 143 FPB

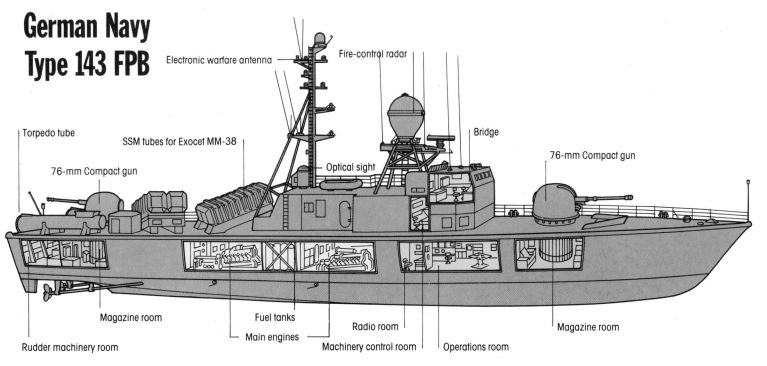

Electronic warfare antenna

Fire-control radar

Torpedo tube

SSM tubes for Exocet MM-38

Bridge

76-mm Compact gun

Optical sight

76-mm Compact gun

Magazine room

Fuel tanks

Radio room

Magazine room

Rudder machinery room

Main engines

Machinery control room

Operations room

Sparviero hydrofoils, which are underpowered on only 5,044 hp (3,780 kW).

For many years the standard Eastern Bloc diesel was the extremely complicated and unreliable M503. This 42-cylinder engine develops 4,000 hp, and powers Soviet P.6 and Komars, and Osa Is, as well as most Chinese and other Communist countries' FPBs. Two M503s driving a common gearbox are used in the Nanuchkas. The M503 is basically seven 6-cylinder aircraft-type radial engines connected together on a common shaft. The 56-cylinder M504 powering the Osa II and its derivatives adds two more rows to increase the maintenance nightmare for an extra 1,000 hp (750 kW). A variety of simpler modern diesels and gas turbines are used on the latest vessels.

A feature on some larger modern Western-built boats, such as the 170-184-ft (52-56-m) types built by Vosper Thornycroft is the use of small electric motors for slow-speed manoeuvring and economical slow patrolling.

Gunboats

Many navies need gunboats more for general patrol work than offensive action. At the largest end of the range is the 187-ft (57-m) type designed by Lurssen. This has the same hull as the missile boats (Turkey has both types), but lacks SSMs. The 397 ton (full load) Spanish Lazangas (licence-built by Bazan), for example, have a main armament of one 76 mm OTO Melara DP, plus lighter guns. With two rather than the usual 57-m type's four shafts, they have a reduced maximum speed of almost 30 knots. Another type in this class is the PR 72 design by SFCN of France, as built for Senegal.

Most gunboats are smaller. At 165 tons (full load), the ASI-315 Pacific Patrol Boat, supplied by Australia to six Pacific island states since 1985, was designed as the smallest unit that had the 8-10 days endurance to cover the large areas required. The emphasis is on range (33 tons fuel capacity) and navigational equipment, rather than armament (which is minimal) and speed (20 knots). Most of the smaller Caribbean islands have a similar need for FPBs with minimal military equipment, but with less range and seaworthiness and higher speeds. Seventeen Caribbean, and Central and South American states use adapted 65-120-ft (20-37-m) commercial designs from the USA. There are many other boats in this class, including the French Patras, the USN Swifts, the British-designed Mexican Aztecs, and the various 65-110-ft (20-34-m) boats built by Vosper Thornycroft, Brooke Marine and Fairey.

The Eastern Bloc equivalent is the Zhuk class, designed originally for the Coastal Patrol branch of the KGB. This 79-ft (24-m), 60-ton (full load) FPB is used by 16 navies in all parts of the world, and is normally armed with two twin 14.5-mm machine guns. Of all the simple gunboats, the most unsophisticated is the Shanghai type, built in China and (under licence) in Romania. Used by 16 navies, the longer-hulled Shanghai

II is still being constructed, despite first appearing in 1961. These have a heavier armament (usually two twin 37-mm and two twin 25-mm plus some ASW weapons) than most others in this class.

Owners

Since 1945, most FPBs have been owned by major powers for defence, such as the pre-1980s Chinese, or by smaller navies with either a limited budget or limited strategic aims. Almost all countries, however, own a few, if only to promote export sales, or because – as with the French – there are still some colonial possessions to police. Even so, there are some countries that do not have any. They include The Netherlands and Belgium; Britain has some for training and for the Royal Naval Reserve. As needs change, so FPBs are acquired or discarded. The USA is debating the value of its Pegasus PHMs, but retains smaller craft for its Special Forces.

There is a concentration of large boats in certain parts of the world that are well-suited to FPB operations – the Gulf, the Baltic, the South Pacific and the Mediterranean, plus some parts of South America. The prime locations are enclosed waters where larger warships do not have sufficient room to make best use of their capabilities.

Some countries – particularly the oil-rich states in the Gulf and in Central America – can afford the boat or the missile they want, but others have to make do and

mend. For example, the many navies that have received Osas either as free transfers or at knockdown prices are faced with a problem replacing them. All are more than 20 years old, and neither the USSR

Right: A naval unit of the Chinese People's Liberation Army patrolling waters in Shanghai-class Fast Patrol Boats (FPBs). These vessels were designed and built by China, as were the Hainan-class FPBs. Other Chinese FPB designs, however, have mainly followed those of the Soviets. A number of these have been steel-hulled variants of the P.6 type, but the Chinese have made direct copies of the Soviet Osa 1 type, still the most numerous SSM-armed FPBs in service.
Below: A Soviet Navy Osa 1 with three of its missile tubes visible.

nor China have built the numbers of missile boats needed to replace them, even on a one for three or four basis. Modern Soviet FPBs – the Nanuchkas and then the Tarantuls – are much larger and more expensive to buy and run. Western equipment is even more expensive, as the Egyptians have discovered in the recent re-equipment of their FPB force. The result is a gradual diminution of SSM-armed navies in the developing world, and a growth in practical, affordable gunboats.

A number of second-rank navies retain a powerful influence in FPB design. The Israelis, with their extensive combat experience and well-defined offensive requirements, have produced a family of Lurssen-based developments that match their needs. They have a mix of sizes – from anti-terrorist patrol boats to mini-corvettes capable of reaching Libya – and of armaments. The missile boats have a mix of Harpoon OTH and Gabriel shorter-range SSMs with a variety of guidance systems to overwhelm opponents.

The Scandinavian countries also have their own specialities. Norway, faced with a superpower in a terrain unsuited to conventionally guided anti-ship missiles, devised a force armed with its own solution – the Penguin SSM. Sweden, in the potentially even more hostile Baltic, retains considerable faith in the surface attack torpedo, and has devised – in the RBS-15 – an even more effective SSM. From the Spicas – with their aft-set bridge to give a clear field of fire – onwards, they have been justifiably obsessed with the problem of air-attack, and have designed their boats accordingly. They also have the unique 'hangars' cut in cliffsides out of solid rock, where warships up to the size of destroyers can safely ride out even nuclear explosions.

Different parts of the world have different needs. In the Caribbean, seaworthiness and range are generally less important than speed, whereas for states such as Chile or Peru the opposite is the case. For the Central Pacific islands, with their extensive territories, military qualities are far less important than adequate endurance and superb navigational equipment.

For some countries, there are restrictions that linger from the past. For example, even though – like Sweden – the Finnish Navy considers the torpedo a useful weapon for surface attack, Finland cannot, under the terms of a 1947 peace treaty with the USSR, have torpedo boats, or submarines, although the USSR was the first to sell Finland the modern equivalent – the SSM-armed FPB.

Typical boats

When the British defence review of November 1956 recommended abolishing Coastal Forces and restricted developments to trials and training, it looked as though Britain had opted out of the FPB market. Several British yards thought differently, and exports remained buoyant. Following the demise of Brooke Marine in the early 1980s Vosper Thornycroft (VT) became the major British FPB builder. Fairey Marine, now Fairey Marinenteck, is the other significant current British builder with the 70-ft (21-m) Tracker and 85-110-ft (26-34-m) Protector types.

Most of the smallest craft are built for paramilitary forces such as police and customs, but since the early 1960s VT 103-ft (31-m) and 110-ft (33-m) boats have been sold to ten navies and the US Coast Guard, which is buying 37 of the 110-ft type. These are being built under licence as the Island-class cutters between 1985-90 by the Bollinger yard in Lockport, Louisiana, USA. Displacing 165 tons full load, and powered by two 2,910-hp (2,180-kW) Paxman Valentia diesels built by Alco in the USA, they have a top speed of 29.7 knots and an armament of 1×20 mm, 2×40 mm grenade launchers and $2 \times$ mgs. This is light compared with the Singapore variant, which has either 1×40 mm or 1×76 mm forwards. The Islands are more angular than earlier 103- and 110-ft VT boats, which had a handsome outline with a prominent funnel. They have a total crew of 16.

Two classes of an enlarged 120-ft (37-m) design were built in the 1970s for Venezuela and Brunei, but the larger modern boats are based on the 220 tons full load 144-ft (44-m) Tenacity, which was built as a private venture by VT in 1967-69, when it became apparent that modern missiles and electronics would demand much larger boats. It was eventually bought by the Royal Navy in 1972, and used for fishery protection duties, but the design was enlarged to produce first the six 312-tons full load 170-ft (52-m) Egyptian Ramadan class, then the 425-ton full load 186-ft (56.7-m) Kenyan Province and Omani Dhofar classes, and most recently the similar-sized Vita type.

The six Ramadans, built between 1978 and 1982, have four MTU 20V-538-TB91 diesels, each producing 4,250 hp (3,190 kW), giving a maximum speed of 37 knots. They are armed with four Otomat Mk 1 SSM ($2 \times$ twin launchers) amidships, 1×76 mm OTO Melara Compact gun forwards, and 2×40 mm Breda/Bofors guns ($1 \times$ twin) aft. There is a crew of 31 officers and men. Their most significant feature is their extensive fit of sensors, and the integrated operations room, something impossible to work into the 83-ft (25.3-m) 6 October class which VT was fitting out as reduced versions of the Ramadan at the same time. The Ramadans have two Marconi surveillance radars, two Marconi tracking radars with slaved TV cameras, a separate optical director, Racal-Decca EW equipment, and a British Aerospace gun-control system.

Left: A scantly armed 105-ft FPB, built by Swiftships Inc., Louisiana, used by the Costa Rican Navy for coastal patrol. In the Caribbean, speed is more important than firepower and seaworthiness. By contrast, the Ramadan-class fast missile attack craft (right) of the Egyptian Navy is 107 ft long and well-armed. This vessel is not really in the FPB class, having a deepened hull forwards to give two decks and greater seaworthiness. The modification also gives a much enlarged arms capacity.

Surface-to-Surface Missile

Exocet (France)

MM-38
Length: 17 ft (5.2 m); Weight: 1,620 lb (735 kg); Warhead: 360 lb (165 kg); Speed: Mach 0.93; Range: 25 nautical miles (46 km); Terminal cruise height: sea skimming; Solid-fuel rocket. Guidance: active radar fire-and-forget.

Most widely used Western FPB SSM. MM.38 entered service in 1974.

MM 40
In service from 1981. Longer body – 19 ft (5.8 m) – and improved range – about 35 nautical miles (56 km), with modified homing system. Increased weight – 1,875 lb (850 kg) – more than offset by using glass fibre rather than metal launch tube, saving about 1,220 lb (600 kg) and considerable volume per missile.

Gabriel (Israel)
Mk 1 – Length: 11 ft (3.35 m); Weight: 950 lb (430 kg); Warhead: 220 lb (100 kg); Speed: Mach 0.7; Range: c.12 nautical miles (22 km); Terminal cruise height: sea skimming; Solid-fuel rocket; Guidance: semi-active radar command.

In service from 1971-72, a much needed riposte to Styx. Mk 1 version was short ranged and command guidance system caused problems with engaging multiple targets.

Mk 2 – same systems as Mk 1, but longer body – 11.2 ft (3.4 m) – with improved fuel for extra range – about 22 nautical miles (41 km).

Mk 3 – completely reworked missile with enlarged warhead – 330 lb (150 kg) – some Mk 1 hits had failed to sink OSAs. Even longer body – 12.5 ft (3.8 m) – and variety of guidance options including fire-and-forget, command and semi-active homing, and mid-course guidance, plus better ECCM systems.

South Africa and Taiwan build Mk 1 under licence as Skorpioen and Hung Feng respectively. Taiwan has a Mk 2 with modified infra-red terminal guidance.

Harpoon RGM-84A (USA)
Length: 12.9 ft (3.93 m); Weight: 1,470 lb (667 kg); Warhead: 500 lb (227 kg); Speed: Mach 0.85; Range: 70 nautical miles (130 km); Terminal cruise height: sea skimming; Turbojet. Guidance: active radar fire-and-forget.

The standard USN anti-ship missile, in service since 1977. Extremely sophisticated electronics. Export refused to several countries, including Taiwan. When Israel transferred two Reshefs and two Sa'ars to Chile, Harpoon SSMs were removed. The Standard Arm was fitted as an interim SSM to some Ashevilles.

Penguin (Norway)
Mk 1 – Length: 9.8 ft (3 m); Weight: 750 lb (340 kg); Warhead: 265 lb (120 kg); Speed: Mach 0.8; Range: 16 nautical miles (30 km); Terminal cruise height: sea skimming; Solid-fuel rocket. Guidance: infra-red homing, programmable inertial guidance system (INS). Small, relatively cheap and very reliable. In service since 1971. Designed for use in the fjords and islands of Norway, hence the programmable INS. Mk 2 with improved electronics developed with Sweden. Mk 3 has increased range – 20+ nautical miles (40+ km).

RBS-15 (Sweden)

Length: 14.25 ft (4.35 m); Weight: 1,720 lb (780 kg); Warhead: N/A; Speed: Mach 0.8+; Range: 40+ nautical miles (70+ km); Terminal cruise height: sea skimming; Turbojet. Guidance: active radar programmable INS.

Entering service in the 1980s. Extremely sophisticated electronics, and can cope with the many islands and hostile EW environment of the Baltic.

SS-12 (France)

Length: 6.1 ft (1.87 m); Weight: 165 lb (75 kg); Warhead: c.66 lb (30 kg); Speed: 210 mph (380 km/h); Range: 3 nautical miles (5.5 km); Terminal cruise height: controlled by operator. Guidance: wire-guided.

A very inferior replacement for a torpedo, this became the first Western SSM in 1968. Totally outclassed, it is being taken out of service.

Styx (USSR)

(SS-N-2A) – Length: 21.3 (6.5 m); Weight: 5,070 lb (2,300 kg); Warhead: 1,100 lb (500 kg); Speed: Mach 0.9; Range: 25 nautical miles (46+ km); Terminal cruise height: 325-980 ft (100-300 m); Liquid-fuel rocket. Guidance: active radar fire-and-forget.

The P-15 SSM – (NATO designation SS-N-2 Styx) – was the first FPB SSM in service anywhere. It was the first to achieve combat success (in 1967) and it is still the most widely used FPB SSM in the world. Design started in 1954, and it entered service on Komars in 1958. There have been three Soviet versions. The original SS-N-2A on the Komars and OSA Is had fixed wings. The –2B introduced on the OSA II boats had folding wings in a smaller, lighter launching tube. Both had an effective range of only about 16 nautical miles due to limitations in the command and guidance system on the FPB.

The current –2C version introduced on Nanuchkas has a lengthened body with more fuel, giving a range of about 45 nautical miles (83 km). It descends to 6-30 ft (1.8-9 m) during the final approach to the target to make it more difficult to detect and shoot down, and has combined radar and infra-red homing to lessen the chances of being decoyed.

The Styx's main advantage is its large warhead, but it is a large, easily detected missile that is vulnerable to countermeasures, especially in its early variants. The Chinese have their own versions: the Hai Ying – 1 (Sea Eagle) is a copy of the SS-N-2A, and several variants have appeared with different guidance and homing systems. They are now producing a number of more advanced SSMs, including the 21.5 nautical miles (40 km) Ying-Ji C801.

Other Soviet FPB SSM

SS-N-9 – Introduced in 1969. Length: 28.8 ft (8.8 m). Same size warhead as Styx, but uses solid fuel. Range: 60 nautical miles (110 km). It is carried by Soviet Navy Nanuchka and Sarancha FPBs as well as Charlie and Papa class nuclear submarines.

SS-N-22 – Used in the Tarantul III FPBs as well as Destroyers. Speed: Mach 2.5; Range: 60 nautical miles (110 km). The latest Soviet SSM.

The French octuple Crotale surface-to-air missile system, as fitted on the Type 62 vessels supplied to United Arab Emirates. The fitting of SAMs on FPBs is a recent development and is the result of increased tension and developments in the Gulf.

Guns

The standard gun is the 76-mm OTO Melara Compact DP (Dual Purpose – ie surface and anti-aircraft). This is fitted on almost all the larger Western-built FPBs, with the Bofors 57 mm as the only major alternative. The 76 mm is fully automatic, with no-one in the turret. The ammunition is fed from a carousel below deck – the Royal Navy calls this the 'bottling factory' because it looks like one. It holds about a minute's ammunition – 85 rounds at 80 rpm, and is refilled by hand. The maximum range is about 7 nautical miles (13 km), but the effective range is about 4.3 nautical miles (8 km) against surface targets.

The newest 'Super Rapid' variant fires at up to 120 rpm, and a 'course-corrected' (ie guided) shell is being developed. Secondary guns (used as main ones on smaller craft) include 40-mm Bofors (also made by Breda), the 30-mm Goalkeeper Gatling, and 30-mm and 20-mm Oerlikons. Soviet boats mostly have twin 30-mm guns, with the newer, larger ones having a 76.2-mm automatic DP gun too. The twin 30 mm was introduced on the OSAs, and many of the more recent Soviet FPBs have the single 30-mm Gatling gun.

Torpedoes

Most navies now use only torpedoes for ASW, but some, especially Sweden, have persisted with the development of wire-guided torpedoes as an effective weapon for attacking surface ships. Sweden, in its Type 61 HTP (High Test Peroxide – Hydrogen Peroxide-fuelled) wire-guided torpedo, has an extremely formidable underwater guided missile. Wakeless, and therefore difficult to detect, it has a 530-lb (240-kg) warhead, and a range of about 16.2 nautical miles (30 km). It is only very recently that missile guidance technology has matched the flexibility of such a torpedo in areas like the Baltic, where the large number of islands and the likelihood of severe electronic and IR jamming make it difficult for missiles to locate their targets.

Surface-to-Air Missiles (SAMs)

A recent development has been the fitting of SAMs on FPBs. Many boats now carry simple mountings for a number of standard man-portable SAMs. For example, many Soviet boats carry SA-N-5 quadruple mountings using Grail missiles, and the Israelis use the American Redeye. The Soviets were the first to fit more capable SAMs on the larger boats, starting with the SA-N-4 twin mounting for Gecko missiles in the Nanuchka class. The Lurssen Type 62s supplied to the United Arab Emirates have the French octuple Crotale SAM launcher, and the six boats built by CNR in Italy for Iraq have the quadruple Albatros launcher for the Aspide SAM. Some of these SAMs, such as the Israeli Barak now being fitted to its existing larger FPBs, can be used against sea-skimming SSMs as well as aircraft.

Electronics and Optronics

Along with the training and competence of the crew, the sensors, command and control systems and electronic warfare equipment are more important in combat than hull, machinery or weapons performance. Modern radars with IFF (Identification Friend or Foe) and optronics (for example, TV cameras, laser rangefinders and IR (Infra-Red) sensors and imagers) allow detection, location and identification of the enemy. The command and control systems handle information coming in so the enemy can be engaged in the optimum way. The electronic warfare systems assist in locating the enemy – Electronic Surveillance Measures (ESM) – defeating the enemy's own weapons – Electronic Counter Measures (ECM) including active jammers and chaff dispensers as well as IR decoys – and enabling the boat's own weapons and sensors to perform against the enemy's ECM – Electronic Counter Counter Measures (ECCM).

The larger the boat, the more comprehensive the equipment that can be fitted if desired, and – more important – if it can be afforded, because this equipment is even more expensive than the weapons. Perhaps the most sophisticated FPB system currently afloat is the West German AGIS automatic command and control system fitted on the Type 143 and 143A FPBs. This has data links that enable the battle to be controlled from their base at Flensburg.

Left: The Ericsson MARIL 880 command, control and information system in the Spica II missile craft. It includes tactical displays and weapons control consol.

Far left: The US-built Shimrit-class hydrofoil FPB bristles a range of electronic aids, together with missiles and guns.
Left: Penguin surface-to-surface missiles launched from a Norwegian fast patrol boat. The missile has a programmable inertial guidance system, designed for use in the fjords and islands of Norway. Hydrofoils have the advantage of high speed with economic fuel consumption, but their performance in rough seas is not good – neither is their stability as a weapons platform.

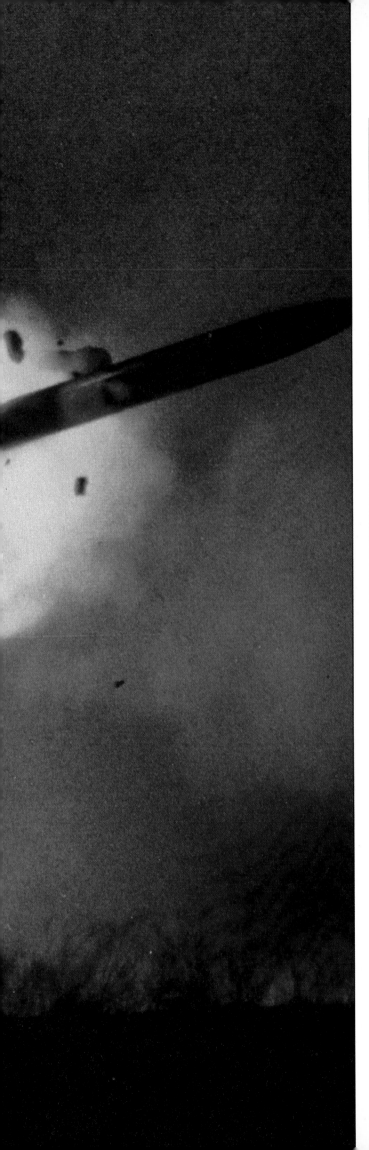

Chapter 6
REGIMENT IN REVIEW:
The Royal Artillery

The Royal Artillery differs from other regiments in having neither colours nor battle honours. The rallying point for a gunner in battle is not a flag but the nearest gun, so the guns are the colour of the Royal Regiment. Battle honours, in a regiment which attends virtually every battle, would be superfluous, so the regiment's badge merely says 'Ubique' (Everywhere).

The disposition of the RA and its sophisticated equipment reflects current defence priorities. For example, the heavy and field regiments are in Germany, as is the missile regiment, forming an important component of NATO's central front; subunits are in the Falklands; and regiments provide troops for internal security duties in Northern Ireland.

Larkhill on Salisbury Plain in England was chosen in the years after World War I as the home of the Royal School of Artillery and quickly became established as the technical focus of the regiment. Men and their machines are put through their paces at Larkhill.

handful of gunners to maintain them. When the need for a field force arose, a train of artillery was taken out of store and attached to the force. The guns appear to have been operated by the ordinary soldiers of line, supervised by the trained gunners, bombardiers and fireworks who were also drawn from the castles and forts as required. Once the campaign was over, the equipment went back into store accompanied by its supervisory staff and the soldiers were dispersed to their original regiments.

This system was adopted for William III's campaigns, and the duration of these – 1689 to 1698 –

Below: Artillerymen in 1807, when the strategies for deploying artillery were still being worked out. The regiment has gone through a series of radical developments, as have the weapons available to them. Always, the battlefield was the testing ground.

Nobody knows who invented the first gun, or when, or where it was invented. The first known written reference is in 1326, and the first record of guns in England is in 1338, when the Clerk of the King's Ships delivered three iron and two brass cannon to the Keeper of the King's Ships for transport to France. Subsequently, at the Battle of Crecy in 1346, one account tells how King Edward 'struck terror into the French Army with five or six pieces of cannon'.

The first mention of a professional artilleryman comes in the Accounts of the Privy Wardrobe which, in November 1375, refer to one William Newlyn as being the King's Master Gunner at Calais, suggesting that the rank of Master Gunner is probably the oldest in the British (or any other) Army.

The first English brass cannon were cast in 1521, and in 1542 the Sussex ironmasters began casting iron cannon. Some of these guns would have been used in the French wars of the period but, in truth, artillery during its first two centuries or so had little effect on the course of battles.

The guns were ponderous. The 'Bastard Culverin' weighed 2,460 lb (1,120 kg) but fired only a mere 7-lb (3-kg) ball. They were slow. It was not uncommon for the damage caused by one shot to be repaired by the enemy before the next shot was fired. And they were relatively immobile. They were emplaced on baulks of timber at the commencement of battle, fired one or two rounds, the foot soldiers and cavalry advanced, and that was the end of the artillery contribution. And once the French wars ended in 1559 the English Navy was sufficient to keep invaders away and the army was neglected in all its branches. When the Civil War broke out, the Roundheads had no guns and the Cavaliers were so ignorant of the use of those they had that they were of little practical value.

The organization of artillery in this period was haphazard. A number of coastal forts and castles held guns emplaced to deal with attacks from the sea, although most of these were in poor condition. Other forts and castles held 'trains of artillery', together with a meant that Marlborough was able to impose some degree of organization into companies and regiments, and the artillery in the field performed very well. At the end of the war, in May 1698, King William III issued a warrant for the retention of a permanent regimental train of artillery, largely to provide employment and reward for some of the men who had served in the various trains during the war.

Instead of merely keeping a collection of guns and wagons and half-a-dozen men to look after them, the entire train was kept in being, complete with the men necessary to serve the guns in case of war. The train was divided into four companies of varying strengths and was specifically ordered 'to be kept in pay in time of peace'. This was the first regular artillery force in England.

The train was reduced in strength in 1699 but, having established such a force it was a logical progression to regularize it as a regiment in its own right, so in 1716 the Royal Regiment of Artillery was authorized, its two 'marching companies' being quartered at Woolwich, the home of the regiment ever since.

Although the trains contained the men necessary to work the guns, they did not contain the horses and drivers to move them; these still had to be hired as and when they were needed. This was standard practice throughout Europe at that time, and it led to several near-disasters. At Fontenoy in 1745, the civilian drivers deserted with their teams as soon as battle loomed and the infantry had to drag the guns forward so that both foot and guns arrived late. A similar fate befell a Prussian battery attacked by Russian cavalry at Zorndorf.

The guns were still heavy and slow, and the gunners marched alongside them – a practice that was satisfactory for supporting the infantry, but useless for cavalry. In 1793 the Royal Horse Artillery was formed – a fully mounted unit using light guns, which could keep up with the cavalry in the approach march and deploy rapidly when necessary. Light mountain guns were added during the Napoleonic Wars, for service in the Peninsula, although these did not become a regular part of the artillery organization.

After the Napoleonic Wars the artillery was again diminished in size and did not revive until the Crimean War. Up to this point, an artilleryman from Marlborough's army could have been dropped into a Napoleonic or even later gun position and would have found little that was unfamiliar to him. The guns were still muzzle-loading smoothbores, using gunpowder and round shot, and the gunners still fired at what they could see, over open sights. But the Crimean War took place in the aftermath of the Industrial Revolution when in Britain there were numerous engineers and inventors looking for new worlds to conquer. To them the war provided a stimulus.

Hitherto, wars had taken place a long way from England, and were ill-reported. The Crimea was still a long way off but it was connected by telegraph, and

Above: Cannon and mortars of the early 16th century – when the first English brass cannon were cast. These guns and others of the period were used in the French wars, but they had little effect then.

there was a *Times* reporter on the spot who was not backward in commenting on the deficiencies of the army. One result of this was to bring William Armstrong, a Newcastle engineer, into the gun-making business, after which guns were never the same.

Armstrong developed the first practical breech-loading gun, using a rifled barrel, built up from a series of wrought iron tubes. Each tube was machined to a precise size and shrunk on to the tube beneath to form a reinforced gun barrel. He then went on to develop projectiles and fuzes for the rifled gun.

Rifling a barrel required skilled engineering but the advantages made the cost and effort worthwhile. There were three advantages. Firstly, the rifling spun the projectile so that it followed a good line and improved accuracy. Secondly, the projectile of a rifled barrel can be elongated, instead of spherical, so it can be made heavier for a given calibre. Thirdly, the layering technique made the gun lighter and stronger than a cast-iron piece. The field and horse batteries were rapidly converted to the new Rifled Breech-Loading (RBL) Armstrong guns, and the coast defences and Royal Navy began to follow suit.

In 1859, however, came a scare over the French

construction of an iron-clad warship. It was thought highly likely that Napoleon III, in one of his more belligerent moods, might well despatch a fleet of these vessels across the English Channel to attack British naval bases and ports. As a result a massive programme of fort construction was put under way, and trials of guns were begun to determine the best method of defeating iron-clad ships.

It was soon discovered that to propel a shot with sufficient force to smash through iron armour, a heavy and powerful gun was required. And the Armstrong breech-closing system was not strong enough to withstand the enormous cartridges required for this task. So in the early 1860s the design of guns reverted to muzzle-loading, abandoning breech-loading but retaining the Armstrong built-up construction and the advantages of rifling. It was not until 1880 that a stronger system of breech-loading was developed by Armstrong and new BL guns began to appear. But Rifled Muzzle-Loading (RML) guns remained in the coast defences until the turn of the century.

From the Crimea to the turn of the century there was relatively little action for the artillery, the succession of small wars requiring no more than a handful of field or horse batteries. On the other hand the expansion of coast defences, required by the installation of coaling stations throughout the Empire, led to an increase in garrison companies. It was the practice at that time to post men indiscriminately to field or garrison duty, and for officers to make tours of duty in field or garrison posts in turn.

The isolation of some of the garrison stations – including St Lucia, Mauritius, Tasmania or even No Man's Land Fort in the Solent – made service there unpopular and was regarded as punishment. Those posted there made no attempt to conceal their displeasure and were simply filling in time until they returned to the field branch where, they thought, there were better opportunities for action and promotion. So in 1899 it was decided to split the regiment into two components; the field force and the garrison force.

The Royal Garrison Artillery and the Royal Field Artillery separated. There were complicated rules about how to determine who went where, but on the whole it worked well and once firmly established as Garrison or Field, the officers and men settled down to make their career in their particular branch.

The South African War came hard on the heels of this reorganization and demanded an enormous expansion in men and in artillery. The men were found from various places, but the equipment could not be produced by British gunmakers fast enough, and one division's worth of field guns was bought secretly from Germany.

Once in South Africa, the gunners, like the rest of the army, discovered that their training simply did not fit the tactical requirements. The deployment of artillery was largely based on the tactics that were effective in the Franco-Prussian War of 1870. The artillery was

deployed in the open and first attacked the enemy's artillery, then prepared the ground for the infantry by bombarding the enemy position selected for attack.

It was considered that for this tactic to succeed, it was necessary to bring into action the maximum number of guns as quickly as possible. But it was soon discovered that such action simply attracted a torrent of shells and bullets from unseen guns and rifles, decimating the artillery before it could begin to fire. The Boers, it appeared, had not studied the same drill book as the rest of the world's armies. And armed with rifles and artillery firing smokeless powder from concealed positions, they had it all their own way.

The Boers also astonished the British by their bold use of long-range guns. Hitherto the criterion for a gun's excellence was its power, its ability to throw a heavy shell to a useful range. The Boers exploited the range, usually out-ranging the British guns, and it was not until Naval 4.7-inch, 5-inch and 6-inch guns were removed from ships and mounted on extemporized field carriages that this threat was countered.

Altogether, the South African War was a valuable training ground. The field artillery rapidly learned to

deploy in concealed positions and use indirect fire. For this it had to deploy observers and develop methods of communicating between observers and guns. New instruments and sights had to be devised and rules were drawn up for the conduct of fire. Howitzers, previously neglected, became invaluable for dropping shells into concealed positions which gun shells and rifle bullets could not reach, because of their flat trajectory. New organizational systems were also devised, to allow more than one battery of artillery to function as a unit.

After the South African War the first priority was to develop new guns, particularly for the field artillery. Specifications were drawn up and sent out to the principal gunmakers as well as to Woolwich Arsenal, and the resulting designs were carefully tested. To incorporate the best features, a hybrid using an Armstrong gun, a Vickers recoil system and the Woolwich carriage was selected as the 18-pounder field piece. A similar, smaller, hybrid was selected as the 13-pounder RHA gun. Even as these were being approved, the Russo-Japanese War brought some more lessons to be studied, and one result of this was the development of a heavy 9.2-inch howitzer to bombard defensive positions.

Dangerous approaches

Another potential war machine which appeared at this time was the aeroplane, and the Royal Artillery began considering methods for attacking aircraft. Evidence of the forward thinking of some people at the time is the suggestion from a Major Hawkins which appeared in the Proceedings of the RA Institute in 1913:

'. . . had we kept our proper place in the van of scientific progress by judicious expenditure in the past

Above: The Royal Horse Artillery (RHA) during the Boer War in 1900. At the beginning of the war, the artillery was heavily depleted, as is usual in inter-war years. This campaign, however, had unusual challenges, coming after the regiment was reorganized into the Royal Garrison Artillery and the Royal Field Artillery. The war was a valuable turning point in the evolution of strategies for artillery, and many lessons were learned from it. Right: Mantlets at Barracks Battery during the Siege of Sebastopol in the Crimean War, which preceded the Boer War.

few years, we might well have mobile aerial torpedoes, worked by wireless currents, which would make the approaches to our dockyards as dangerous to dirigibles . . . as the 3-mile limit is to hostile ships of war . . .'

In the absence of aerial torpedoes, guns had to do the job, and in 1913 the first Anti-Aircraft (AA) gun trials were conducted on the Isle of Wight, using a one-pounder pom-pom to fire at a kite towed at speed by a destroyer. At the same time, designs for a 3-inch AA gun were put in hand.

At the outbreak of war in 1914 the Royal Artillery consisted of 26 batteries of horse (13-pr gun) and 153 of field (18-pr gun and 4.5-in howitzer) artillery, 87 Garrison Companies, 12 heavy batteries (60-pr guns), nine mountain batteries (10-pr guns) and three siege batteries (6-inch 30-cwt howitzers) in the regular force, and 14 horse, 151 field, 76 Garrison Companies, 20 heavy batteries and three mountain batteries in the Territorial Army.

The Garrison Companies manned the coast defences and a high proportion of the remainder of the regular force was on service in India. Horse and field batteries accompanied the British Expeditionary Force to France, where they were soon in the thick of the Retreat from Mons. At this stage of the war the old-time habits still prevailed, and the guns were often dispersed among the front-line infantry. They wanted not only to give support, but to be *seen* to be giving support, and the moral effect was considered to be highly important. To this end, 121 Field Battery, near Frameries, had two guns actually in the Dorset Regiment's firing line, firing over open sights at German machine guns at a range of no more than 750 yds (820 m).

The culmination of this exposed, toe-to-toe, type of artillery fighting came at Le Cateau on August 26, when almost the entire Corps artillery was deployed in a long line across a forward slope, their orders being simply to stop the German advance. As the first German troops met this blocking position, they called up their own artillery, which moved into position some 5,000 yds (4,570 m) away. A murderous duel began, and because of the advanced position of the guns, any German shell which missed the artillery inevitably hit the accompanying infantry. In spite of immense sacrifice, the advance of the German Army could only be checked, not halted, and eventually the battered British Force had to retire. But its action had bought time for the remainder of the Allied armies and proved to be a crucially important battle of the war.

This battle also provided an important lesson: no longer would guns be placed in front among the infantry, but would be dispersed in concealed positions in depth, so that they could provide fire without attracting it to themselves. Equally important, that battle firmly cemented the mutual respect of the infantry and artillery, each having seen the other in action at close quarters, which was to remain throughout the war.

New demands

By the end of 1914 the trench lines had been established from the North Sea to the Swiss border, and the war took on the nature of a siege, with the Allies attempting to break into the fortress that was Germany. This attack required not only more artillery but a much greater proportion of heavy artillery. One medium or heavy gun to every two field guns was the decision, so that the field and horse artillery could deal with close targets posing a direct threat to the infantry while the heavier weapons could destroy defences, attack deeper targets and destroy opposing artillery.

As the war progressed, so various tactical demands were made on artillery, and they could be met only by introducing new types of equipment. In 1914 the standard projectile of field artillery was the shrapnel shell – a supreme killer against troops in the open. By 1915, however, the enemy's troops were no longer in the open, but were concealed in trenches and dugouts; now the need was for high-explosive shells

Left: Artillerymen loading a 15-inch howitzer in France during World War I. Horse and field batteries accompanied the British Expeditionary Force to France. In the early stages of the war, the tactic for deploying the artillery was to disperse them among the front-line of infantry, where they could be seen to be supporting the infantry, who, unfortunately, were hit by return fire.
Right: Artillery deployed during World War I.

and a reduction in the proportion of shrapnel. The need to conceal troop movements led to a demand for smoke shells; the need to see in No Man's Land at night led to illuminating shells, and when gas became a weapon of war the gas shell made its appearance.

The solitary 9.2-inch howitzer, still under trial in 1914, was soon put into full production and was then augmented by 8-inch and 12-inch heavy howitzers; the 6-inch howitzer was improved and issued in large numbers, a 6-inch long-range gun appeared, and, largely by the initiative of gun-makers such as Vickers and Armstrong, heavy naval 9.2-inch, 12-inch and 14-inch guns were mounted on railway trucks and became the super-long-range bombardment weapons.

To detect enemy artillery, aerial photography was perfected and two entirely new techniques were introduced: flash spotting and sound ranging. Flash spotting involved deploying a string of skilled observers across the front to watch for the muzzle flash of guns and measure their bearing. The precise time of the flash, together with the bearing, was reported to a plotting room which, working from several bearings taken at the same instant, could pin-point enemy guns to very close limits. The technique of sound ranging, involved burying microphones in surveyed lines along the front. The sound wave of an enemy gun firing would cross these lines, and reach the microphones at slightly different times. By mathematical analysis of the time differences, it was possible to deduce a bearing from each pair of microphones. These bearings, when plotted on a map, could identify an enemy gun position to an accuracy of about 50 yds (46 m).

The normal method of engaging a target was by eye. An observer forwards in the front line would spot a likely target, deduce its map reference and signal it to the guns. They would calculate the bearing and elevation to hit the target then fire one round. The observer on seeing where this round landed, reported what correction was needed to bring the fall of shot on

to the target, and another round was fired. This procedure continued until the ranging round was in the target area, then the order was given to engage.

The technique was adequate for targets close to the front line and within the observer's sight. But enemy guns concealed behind a crest, or supply dumps some miles behind the line, were out of sight of a ground observer. For such targets, aerial observation was required but it exposed the observer virtually as a sitting duck. Another solution was to engage by 'predicted fire'. This involved calculating the bearing and range from the gun to the target and then applying corrections to compensate for wind, temperature, the difference in height of gun and target, barometric pressure, and various other factors that affect the flight of the shell. At the outbreak of war these 'corrections of the moment' were little understood, and the technique of predicted fire had to be learned by trial and error.

The anti-aircraft engagement was also one that had to be learned the hard way. Here was a target capable of rapid movement in three dimensions. The difficulty was compounded by the time lag between firing the shell and its arrival at the target – a lag during which large movements could occur. Complex sights were developed to compensate for these movements, but they became so involved that some guns had half-a-dozen gunlayers gathered around them, leaving scarcely any room for loading and firing.

Eventually it was recognized that the 'central post' system was best. In this system a central observation post did the sighting and calculation then called the results to the guns. There was also the problem of how to warn the gunners that a target was approaching. The only physical indication of an approaching aircraft was the sound of its engine, and huge 'ear trumpet' sound detectors were developed. Unfortunately, sound travels relatively slowly, and by the time an aircraft 2 miles (3.2 km) away, say, was heard, its speed had brought it appreciably nearer.

The one major tactical lesson that emerged from the war was the need to command artillery from as high a level as possible so as to co-ordinate its fire. The old method of allowing each battery to find its own target and fire on it, without much reference to what the remainder of the army was doing, was no longer relevant. Individual batteries could, and did, fire on 'targets of opportunity', but to demolish some German defensive positions it became necessary to bring to bear the fire of many batteries on one spot, and this demanded a high degree of control. Fire planning – the development of barrages to assist infantry forward or to deny ground to an enemy – became normal, and operations without careful fire planning invariably failed.

On the move

The greatest difficulty, and one which was never really solved, was that of keeping control of artillery during mobile operations. World War I was a war in which it was particularly difficult for the commanders to keep their grip of the commanded once battle began.

Prior to 1914, operations were usually small enough that command could be exercised by voice or runner, and the commander could see what was happening. After 1918, radio and other types of communication were developed. But between those dates the lack of efficient communications meant that the only way to operate was to draw up careful timetables in the hope that the various units could keep to them. Only in this way could the commander begin to have any idea of what various forces might be doing at any time. And once the battle began to move, control was entirely lost. The problem was not peculiar to the artillery; the entire army suffered from it to greater or lesser degrees, but it seemed to hamper artillery operations more than those of other arms.

When the war ended the strength of the Royal Artillery stood at 29,990 officers and 518,790 men, comprising 50 RHA and 876 field batteries, 42 Garrison Companies, 117 heavy, 401 siege, 21 mountain and 289 anti-aircraft batteries. Between them they manned 3,875 guns, 2,562 howitzers, 2,519 mortars and 236 anti-aircraft guns in France alone, and had fired a grand total of 170,385,295 shells during the course of the war.

The immediate post-war years brought about an immense reduction in the strength of the British Army, which was reflected in the reduced strength of the artillery, but there was a determination to extract the utmost benefit from the many lessons that had been learned in France and other theatres of war. Prior to 1914 the School of Gunnery had been in Shoeburyness and attended by a small proportion of gunners; now a new School of Artillery was founded in Larkhill, on Salisbury Plain, and this immediately became the technical focus of the regiment.

At Larkhill the actions of the war were discussed and analysed, doctrines were developed and a Gunnery Staff of instructors was trained, then dispersed to the

various regiments and batteries to impart the new teaching. The development of communications systems, methods of fire control and systems of command were all pursued during the 1920s and 1930s. All systems were tried, changed and retried or discarded.

While the rest of the army contemplated what they could do with the tank, the RA studied methods of stopping tanks and, even by the middle 1920s, were writing into the specifications of new guns a requirement for anti-tank shooting. Anti-aircraft gunnery was also closely examined, new techniques explored and new guns designed. Although the political and economic climate prevented much hardware from being produced, the policies and tactics were worked out so that when funds became available the gunners would be prepared to put their new equipment into service.

Reunited

One major step, taken in 1924, was to bring the Regiment back into one unit, abolishing the distinction between Field and Garrison artillery. The war had shown that the division was no longer valid because Garrison Companies had dragged heavy guns through the Flanders mud alongside field batteries and, indeed, it became apparent that a tractor and 6-inch howitzer was more mobile than an 18-pr gun and a team of horses in such conditions.

The other major step, which took place across the 1930s, was the mechanization of the Regiment, part of the general mechanization of the whole army. As early as 1928 there was an efficient self-propelled gun – the Birch Gun, an 18-pr on a Vickers chassis – but this fell into the pit which yawned between the Royal Tank Regiment and its more vociferous enthusiasts and the rest of the army at that time. By 1932 the Birch Gun was withdrawn and scrapped.

In 1934 the RA had a strength of 2,225 officers and 28,654 men, manning 14 RHA, 112 field, 4 heavy and 25 coast defence batteries. There were also 580 Territorial Army field and medium batteries, plus an element devoted to AA or coast defence, although, in fact, there were few AA guns. It was about this time that the rise of Germany began to make itself apparent and the need for rearmament with modern equipment became pressing.

One of the technical questions arising after the war had been the need for a new field gun to replace the ageing 18-pr. What was needed was something with longer range, a heavier shell and the ability to act either as a gun or as a howitzer, so that it could also replace the 4.5-inch howitzer. Several designs were tried, the first solutions were aimed at providing two weapons – generally a 3-inch gun and a 4.1-inch howitzer, and it was not until 1933 that the gun-howitzer concept took firm hold.

A pilot model was produced in 1934. It was a 3.7-inch weapon, but, in deference to the financial constraints, this was changed to 3.45-inch calibre so that the barrel could be removed from the existing 18-pr guns and the new 3.45-inch barrel inserted, to save the cost of new carriages. This weapon became the '25-pr Mark I' or, as it was universally known, the 18/25-pr, and conversions began to appear in 1936. At the same time, the design of a completely new gun and carriage was put in hand, to be produced when the country could afford it.

For the AA defences, a new 3.7-inch gun designed by Vickers was approved in 1937 and the first guns were delivered in 1938. At that time anti-tank (AT) defence was considered to be an infantry responsibility, but in 1938 the infantry rebelled, saying they had enough to do without that, so the RA was called upon to produce AT batteries to man the new 2-pr gun which had appeared in 1936. The gunners soon realised that the capabilities of this weapon were being rapidly overtaken by contemporary tank design and set about developing a 6-pr gun. The design was completed in 1938, but after making a prototype and testing it, the design had to be shelved for lack of finance and manufacturing facilities.

The medium artillery, the 60-pr gun and 6-inch howitzer, were also elderly and lacking in performance, and replacement was promised in the shape of a new 5.5-inch gun-howitzer. Design of this began in 1939, but there were technical problems and it was not until May 1942 that the first guns were in use. As a result both the 60-pr and the 6-inch howitzer remained in service throughout the war.

Heavy artillery was considered outdated when the Royal Air Force assured everyone that whatever heavy artillery could do, the RAF could do better. With some relief the gunners shelved the heavy artillery requirement and spent the money on more field and AA guns. When war came, however, the RAF were otherwise employed than in support of the army, so heavy artillery had to be obtained from the USA, there being no time for the process of design and development.

Rearmament

The rearmament programme and the need to flesh out the army caused the strength of the Territorial Army to double, and the regular army began to increase in size, particularly when conscription was introduced in 1939. The Royal Artillery took its share of this increase, because it had to man the new anti-tank batteries, the expanding number of AA batteries and the expanding number of field batteries, as well as continuing to man the coast defences. Moreover, the expansion of the army demanded men for sound ranging, flash spotting, artillery intelligence and many other peripheral aspects of artillery which were the result of changes in technique and organization. By the time the Regiment reached its peak, in early 1944, almost one-third of the British Army wore the RA cap badge, and the manpower shortage had resulted in the adoption of 'Mixed AA Batteries' manned by gunners and by women of the ATS. The women performed the less physically demanding duties. Indeed, many of them were convinced that they could have fired the guns as well, given the chance.

In addition to the roles already understood at the outbreak of war, the Regiment found several new ones. Defensively Equipped Merchant Ships (DEMS) carried guns, for both air and sea defence, manned by gunners of the Maritime Regiment RA; gunner officers flew Air Observation Post aircraft, spotting for the guns; airborne gunners descended by parachute or glider and operated 75-mm howitzers and 6-pr anti-tank guns; self-propelled field and anti-tank guns were adopted; radar became the early-warning and gun-directing system for AA guns and coast guns, and was also adapted to detect mortar bombs in flight and to calculate their trajectory; flight rockets were adopted and used, first as AA barrage weapons, then as field bombardment weapons.

The radio link

The most significant change was the widespread adoption of radio communication, enabling commanders to know what their units were doing and to send orders rapidly. Radio allowed observers to bring fire to bear rapidly and to supply headquarters with up-to-date information about events at the front. But, more importantly, by linking regiments together, radio made it possible for any observer at the front to call for specific levels of artillery fire to match the target.

Normally, an observer had only his own battery at his disposal. If circumstances warranted, however, he could call on the fire of the entire regiment, the division, corps, even the entire army, provided the formations were within range of the target. And thanks to radio and the adoption of standardized fire-control procedures, the response time was minimal. A regiment of 24 field guns could be directed on to a target within three

Below: The L118 105mm light gun has a sustained rate of fire of 3 rounds a minute and a maximum range of 10.7 miles (17.2 km). It can be helicopter transported.

L 118 105mm Light Gun

Hydro-pneumatic recuperator

Breech block

Firing lever

Gun layer's seat

Air reservoir

Barrel

Hydraulic recoil buffer

Balancing gear

Saddle pintle

Tail assembly

Breech mechanism lever

Firing platform

Suspension

Above: Gunners adjust the rigging of a 75 mm pack Howitzer pallet prior to take off for a Rhine crossing at the end of the War.

minutes, and even an army response could be organized within half an hour. It was this control and command, enabling masses of guns to be switched about with ease and precision, which made British artillery technically and tactically superior to any other nation's in the war.

The post-war years

The end of World War II led to the usual reduction in military strength, but the continuation of research was unusual. In the immediate post-war years heavy 5.25-inch AA guns were still being installed around major ports, coast defences were being overhauled and new air defence gun designs were being pursued. At the same time the closing months of the war had produced two new weapons of infinite promise – the atomic bomb and the guided missile, and these had to be followed up. But as far as the Royal Artillery was concerned, the immediate post-war years were 'business as usual'.

The system, as refined and honed throughout the war, was efficient, and in the area of greatest danger, the continent of Europe, would continue to be effective. The remainder of the army returned to what was, in effect, imperial policing, which called for little, if any, artillery support, with the result that artillery tactics and techniques remained static for several years after the war. The Korean War was fought with the same equipment and techniques as was World War II, with only minor improvements in details of fire control.

Technological landmarks

In the late 1950s the prospect of artillery actually using nuclear missiles as field weapons became practical, as did compressing a nuclear device into the confines of a gun projectile. These developments heralded a renaissance of artillery. At first too much was expected. There was talk of artillery with the awesome power of nuclear warheads becoming the decisive arm, leaving armour and infantry merely to find targets and protect the artillery. This phase soon passed and, with the introduction of the US Corporal missile in 1958, the Royal Artillery entered the nuclear battlefield. No longer would it be possible to deploy batteries wheel-to-wheel, or to stack ammunition in piles along roadsides. Such concentrations would simply invite nuclear destruction, so dispersion and concealment became prime subjects for study.

With the arrival of a missile capable of being fired many miles beyond the front line, the acquisition of suitable targets became crucial, and in the early 1960s studies began of the use of reconnaissance drones. The old technique of flash spotting was no longer worthwhile, because modern artillery used flashless propellant.

The middle 1950s saw the beginning of NATO standardization, and one of the subjects was artillery calibres. At that time a replacement for the 25-pr gun was under discussion, and an 87-mm weapon with an unusual anti-nuclear overhead shield was in prototype form. So, too, was a self-propelled 5.5-inch gun on a Centurion tank chassis, but both these designs were scrapped when NATO standardized on 105-mm and 155-mm as their two basic calibres. Neither calibre had ever been a British standard, so it became necessary to

FV-433 Abbot

Loader gets ammunition (separate cartridges and shells) through a door in the back of the turret

Gunner lays the gun on target

Smoke grenade launcher

Double baffle muzzle brake

L13A1 105-mm gun capable of −5 degrees depression, +70 degrees elevation and 12 rounds a minute

Driver uses wide-angle periscope when operating with two-piece hatch closed

Rolls-Royce six-cylinder multi-fuel engine developing 240 bhp (180 kW) to give maximum road speed of 30 mph (48 km/h)

Stowage racks

Idler

Commander – cupola can rotate 360 degrees independently of the turret

Rubber-tyred road wheels

Rubber-padded tracks of cast manganese

Drive sproket

Light steel track guards keep down dust thrown up by tracks

look overseas for suitable weapons. The Italian 105-mm M56 pack howitzer and the US M44 155-mm self-propelled howitzer were hurriedly taken into service until native designs could be developed. The first of these was the Abbot self-propelled 105-mm gun, a completely new design using new and more powerful ammunition which developed a range of 10.6 miles (17 km) and this entered service in 1965.

The next major innovation was the computer, the first of which was under test in 1961. The device occupied a caravan of its own, needed a 27-kW generator and was capable of rather less than today's pocket calculator. But this machine, cumbersome and difficult as it was, pointed the way to developing programmes that could perform the routine survey and fire control tasks much quicker and more accurately than slide rules and mechanical calculators. By the end of the 1960s the Field Artillery Computer, small enough to be carried in a Land Rover, was in service.

The 1960s also saw a swing away from the all-out nuclear warfare scenario. The philosophy of Mutually Assured Destruction (MAD) pointed out that such a conflagration was unlikely, but events in other parts of the world, including the Middle East, Borneo and Vietnam, made it apparent that 'brush fire wars' were likely to break out anywhere at any time, and that what

was needed was a fast response. For this, armoured carapaces to keep out nuclear flash and radiation were not needed, but artillery had to be highly portable and capable of being carried in aircraft or slung beneath helicopters.

The score today

The Royal Artillery as it stands today, at the start of the century's last decade, is enormously reduced from previous establishments, although its firepower is increased by a considerable amount. There are three regiments of RHA, nine field regiments, three heavy regiments, one missile regiment, one Commando regiment, one locating regiment, and three air defence regiments, plus a training regiment, a depot regiment, and a support regiment which provides guns and manpower for the Royal School of Artillery.

The Territorial element provides two field regiments, four air defence regiments, three observation post regiments and one Commando battery. Compared with the 290 regular and 264 Territorial batteries existing in 1914, this count is small but what matters is the vastly improved firepower of the equipment with which today's batteries are armed.

Two RHA regiments and one field regiment are still using the Abbot SP gun, although this has been

Left: The Abbot self-propelled gun provided the British Army of the Rhine with highly mobile artillery with ample fire power during the 1960s and 1970s, but is now in urgent need of replacement.

scheduled for replacement for some years. The replacement will be a 155-mm SP howitzer. It was intended that this should be the SP70, which was to be developed by Britain, Germany and Italy. After several years and tens of millions of pounds, however, this design collapsed and the Vickers AS90 is proposed as the replacement weapon. It is unlikely, therefore, that replacement of Abbot will take place much before 1993.

The Airborne (7th) RHA Regiment, the 29th Commando Regiment and the Territorial field Regiments are equipped with the 105-mm Light Gun. This is the weapon that replaced the 105-mm pack howitzer. It was designed to be air-mobile and can be helicopter-lifted, and it fires the same 105-mm ammunition as does Abbot, thus obtaining the same 10.6-mile range. This is a considerable improvement over the more general NATO standard of the US M101 family of ammunition, which gives a maximum range of just over 7.5 miles (12 km), and it is notable that the US Army and US Marine Corps have recently adopted the Light Gun for use with certain formations, although, to conform to their supply system, they are barrelled so as to fire the US ammunition.

The Light Gun was used to good effect during the 1982 Falklands campaign and, indeed, many observers consider that it was the rapid and accurate fire of this weapon which brought about the final surrender of the Argentine Forces in Port Stanley. Well-sited observation posts allowed every movement within the area to be seen and responded to by 105-mm shells, and it was this inevitability of bombardment following activity which told upon the defenders' morale.

Three field regiments are armed with the 155-mm FH70 howitzer. This excellent weapon was also a tri-national development, but a successful one. It fires a 43.5 kg shell to a maximum range of 14.9 miles (24 km), and with rocket-assisted shells can achieve 18.6 miles (30 km). Normally towed into action by a special vehicle, the gun carriage has a built-in Auxiliary Propulsion Unit (APU) which can drive the gun wheels and thus move the gun itself independently of its vehicle. This is of considerable value in shoot-and-scoot tactics, where, after firing a mission, the gun is immediately moved some distance away clear of the inevitable counter-battery fire.

The remaining field regiments are armed with the US M109 155-mm self-propelled howitzer in its latest M109A2 form. It has a longer barrel than the original equipment and can fire a 94.6-lb (42.9-kg) shell to a maximum range of 11 miles (18 km), or 14 miles (23 km) when firing rocket-assisted shells. A large 'family' of ammunition is available for this howitzer, including conventional high-explosive shells containing remotely

delivered munitions (mines or bomblets dispersed over a target area to combat enemy armour) and the Copperhead laser-guided anti-armour projectile, although not all of these are necessarily in use in British formations. The M109 is an elderly design and its principal virtue is its ready and comparatively cheap availability. If and when the AS90 goes into service, it will greatly out-perform the M109 but financial considerations make it unlikely that the M109s will be replaced for many years to come.

The heavy regiments are armed with a mixture of 175-mm SP guns and 203-mm SP howitzers – both US equipment dating from a period when air-portability was gaining in importance over nuclear protection. As a result, instead of the impressive armoured turret and chassis of the M109, these weapons are little more than a tracked chassis with a gun on top. The 175 mm is now obsolescent; it was never a very good weapon, its only virtue being the ability to fire a heavy 147-lb (67-kg) shell to a range of 52.6 miles (32.7 km), and it was adopted in the absence of anything better.

The 203-mm howitzer, which is mounted on the same chassis as the 175-mm gun, fires a 204-lb (92.5-kg) shell to 15 miles (24 km), or a rocket-assisted shell to 30 km. Both these weapons, however, are about to be replaced by the Multiple Launch Rocket System (MLRS). This is a self-propelled, completely autonomous weapon which moves on tracks and carries a launcher unit with twelve 227-mm rockets. The 677-lb (307-kg) rocket carries 644 dual-purpose shaped charge/fragmentation bomblets which, dispersed over the target area, will penetrate armour or blast exposed personnel with fragments.

The solitary missile regiment is armed with the US Lance ground-to-ground missile. This weighs about 3,300 lb (1,500 kg), moves on a tracked carrier-launcher vehicle and carries a 1,000-lb (454-kg) high-explosive warhead or a 10-kT nuclear warhead to a maximum range of about 75 miles (120 km).

The regular air defence regiments are equipped with the Rapier missile, either in tracked or towed form. This is another weapon which proved its worth in the Falklands campaign. Rapier is optically guided, but it can also be provided with radar guidance to give night and all-weather coverage. It will engage attacking aircraft to a range of 4.3 miles (6.8 km) and a height of 9,800 ft (3,000 m), and the towed equipment is light enough to be lifted into position by a helicopter if necessary. The tracked version is enhanced by having a surveillance radar, a thermally enhanced optical tracker which permits operation in poor light conditions, and a helmet-mounted sighting system which can be slaved to the launcher which then automatically points in whatever direction the commander looks.

The Territorial light air defence regiments are equipped with the shoulder-fired Blowpipe missile. These weapons are also distributed throughout the field and heavy regiments for short-range defence.

Tradition and Ceremony

Despite the sophistication of Space-Age technology, the Royal Artillery still finds time for ceremony and tradition. The most outward and visible sign of this is in the presence of the King's Troop, Royal Horse Artillery, in London.

The Troop was founded in 1808 as the Riding Troop, to provide equitation instruction for the regiment, but its principal function today is to provide a saluting battery for royal occasions and ceremonial Guards of Honour. King George VI took a particular interest in the Troop and it was at his request that its title was changed to The King's Troop. Upon the accession of Her Majesty Queen Elizabeth II, the name was continued, at her request in remembrance of her father.

The King's Troop is most commonly seen performing its famous Musical Ride at shows throughout the country during the summer months. Less often, when the occasion demands, it rides through London to St James' Park to fire a Royal Salute. The guns are the 13-pr horse artillery guns developed after the South African War. Many of them were converted into AA weapons during World War I and then re-converted into their field role for ceremonial purposes. So the gun currently firing blank cartridges in St James' Park might well have fired something far more lethal from the same area in 1915-16.

The King's Troop are fully trained on modern equipment and attend firing practice with modern guns every year, just as any service unit.

The Sovereign displays interest in the activities of all artillery units; the Sovereign is the Captain-General of Artillery. Her Majesty periodically visits various artillery stations, and in 1984 the Royal Artillery of the British Army of the Rhine staged an impressive review at Dortmund for inspection by the Captain-General.

The individual units of the Regiment also observe their own ceremonies and traditions. Here, the emphasis is not on regiments but on batteries, because each battery can trace its history back through a succession of differently numbered batteries to its founding. Many have collected Honour Titles which are proudly borne.

The battery titles all reflect heroism, though it takes different forms. 'Martinique 1809' refers to the capture of Fort Desaix on Martinique from the French. 'The Battleaxe Company' actually refers to the same action, but since they captured a ceremonial French axe, they prefer to be remembered for that – and they solemnly parade it every year on the anniversary of the battle. 'The Broken Wheel Battery' commemorates a battle in India when one gun crashed into a ditch but the gunners, ignoring the damage, manhandled it into action. 'Croix de Guerre' battery commemorates the award of the French medal to the entire battery after some particularly desperate work in 1918.

Not all batteries have honour titles; if everyone had one, they wouldn't be honours. Nevertheless, many batteries celebrate some famous action in their history; 'C' Battery, RHA, for example, celebrates the Battle of Balaclava, when their intervention saved the Heavy Brigade from disaster. And, honour title or none, when the celebration day arrives all work is cancelled, a fête day is declared, there is usually a short religious observance at the hour of the battle, and a good time is had by all.

The Royal Artillery annually parade a French axe captured at Fort Desais in Martinique in 1809.

The ACE Mobile Force

An RAF helicopter transports a 105 mm howitzer during AMF exercises in Portugal. Transportability by this means is considered essential for modern artillery.

One of the less well-known NATO organizations is the ACE Mobile Force (AMF); ACE stands for Allied Commander, Europe, and the AMF is at his personal disposition as a form of flank guard and burglar alarm. It consists of a force of about brigade strength which, uniquely, is composed of small units from every NATO army. They include batteries of artillery, battalions of infantry and squadrons of light armour, all supported by a logistic organization which is similarly composed of soldiers from every army.

The function of the AMF is to be positioned on NATO's borders in any area that appears to be sensitive. Should that border be violated, the AMF will be in the forefront of the action. And because the force is composed of elements from every NATO nation, there can be no argument by any member about whether they are obliged to honour treaty obligations – their troops have been involved.

Within the AMF is an artillery element, and within this is a single battery provided by the Royal Artillery. The battery is relieved periodically, so most field batteries have the duty sooner or later, and it is a duty to which most look forward. A tour with AMF gives more opportunity for day-to-day mixing with other nationalities than virtually any other NATO troop duty, and it brings some welcome changes of scene which do not always come the way of a battery stationed, for example, in Germany as part of the NATO Force.

There is frequent exercising in northern Norway, or in Turkey, the two extreme NATO flanks, which other units rarely see. There is the opportunity to attend artillery exercises in the various member countries, so instead of the routines of Salisbury Plain or the Luneberg Heath, the gunners may find themselves in Sardinia or Portugal or northern Italy.

The AMF battery is always armed with the 105-mm Light Gun, but with a difference. The battery may be sent anywhere within NATO, and it has to rely entirely on the host nation. But the host nation may not stock British ammunition, so each gun is provided with two barrels – one that takes standard British ammunition, and another chambered to fire US standard 105-mm ammunition. The barrel is changed before departure, depending on supplies at the destination.

Skis and studded tyres are held for use in Norway and tropical equipment for use in Turkey. Transport is almost invariably by helicopter, and the batteries of the AMF are highly skilled at hitching up and moving by air. A battery can be shifted 6 miles (10 km) and be in action within half an hour, and a squadron of RAF helicopters forms part of the AMF for this purpose, accompanied by a German squadron.

Batteries from Britain, the USA, Portugal, Italy, Germany, Belgium and The Netherlands make up the AMF artillery element. The common language for the artillery command is English, although individual batteries use their own language within their own lines. Not surprisingly, there is an intense element of competition; each battery looks upon itself as the representative of its country's artillery and strives to out-do the others, resulting in an exceptionally high standard of gunnery.

Chapter 7
FORCES LIFE:
Western officer elite

The three officer training establishments at Sandhurst in Britain, West Point in the USA and Saint-Cyr in France were founded within a few years of one another at the end of the 18th century and the beginning of the 19th. Each was established by far-sighted military planners concerned with the idea of competence. As Napoleon Bonaparte, who set up the French École Spéciale Militaire, said, 'It is the greatest immorality to exercise a profession about which you are ignorant.' All countries with regular armies now have their officer training schools. The days of the gentleman officer who bought his commission by virtue of social rank, and exercised his military obligations, often with less enthusiasm than he devoted to the social whirl and riding to hounds, are long past.

French trainee officers on parade. The French prefer the term 'candidates' to 'cadets', which for them has associations with the regime that existed before the Revolution. Three years at the French École Spéciale Militaire de Saint-Cyr give a rigorous grounding.

oday's army officer learns most of his specialist technical skills after officer training school, once he has joined his regiment or unit. What he gains at officer training school are the basics of modern soldiering, the particularities of leadership, considerable physical fitness and, often, an academic qualification equal to or recognized as a university degree.

The rewards of holding a commission are many. The responsibilities are massive. Officer training schools teach their pupils that 'the buck stops here', and begin the process of equipping them to deal with that potentially awesome prospect.

Royal Military Academy

The earliest specialist training for army officers in Europe was usually for the engineers and the artillery, fields in which new scientific discoveries required particular knowledge. Austria had such a school in the 17th century. France's Polytechnique, which began life as the École de Mars in 1791, and England's Royal Military Academy (RMA), founded by George II in 1741 and located at Woolwich, were both primarily schools of engineering and artillery.

RMA Woolwich, known as the 'Shop', continued to be the training establishment for gentlemen cadets hoping for commissions in the Royal Engineers, the Royal Artillery, and, later, the Royal Signals until 1939.

Until the end of the 18th century, Woolwich provided practically the only professional training for officers in the British Army. As a result, indiscipline was widespread among a young officer corps which could buy both its commissions in the first place, and its promotions later in its career.

In 1799 the Commander in Chief of the Army, the Duke of York, founded a small college for the education of young army officers at High Wycombe. This developed two branches: a senior and a junior. The senior branch, formed at the instigation of a brilliant cavalry officer, Le Marchant, was known as the Staff Training College. In 1801 the government gave approval for a more ambitious establishment, and bought the existing Sandhurst estate for the establishment of a Royal Military College.

The impressive building now known as Old College was completed in 1812, and occupied by the junior branch, to form a school to train gentlemen cadets to take commissions in the cavalry and infantry. In 1861 the senior branch moved into a building on the same estate to become the Staff College. In 1871 the practice of buying commissions was abolished. The Royal Military College Sandhurst also trained officer cadets for the British Indian Army, and, later, the Royal Tank Corps, the Royal Army Service Corps and the Royal Army Ordnance Corps.

Left: Training to develop the skills of keeping low and stalking. In the British Army, specialist skills are developed after officer training.

At the beginning of World War II in 1939, both the Woolwich and Sandhurst establishments were closed down, reopening in 1947 as a single academy – the Royal Military Academy Sandhurst (RMAS).

Sandhurst today

The end of the war was also the end of the term 'Gentlemen Cadets'; now Sandhurst pupils are known as 'Officer Cadets'. The name may have changed, but in many ways the first weeks at Sandhurst, when the raw material is first licked into shape, have remained broadly the same.

The NCO instructors on the Standard Military Course, Sandhurst's main course for non-graduates, still come from the Brigade of Guards. The three main commissioning courses at RMAS are the Standard Military Course (SMC), for non-graduates; the Standard Graduate Course (SGC) for those with university degrees, and the Women's Standard Course (WSC).

The Standard Military Course is three terms long, and officially lasts 42 weeks, although extra adventurous training undertaken during leave brings it up to at least 44 weeks. The Standard Graduate Course is two terms long, lasting some 29 weeks in all. The Women's Standard Course is also of two terms, and runs in parallel with the SGC.

"The girls' course is about the same as the SGC. They work together more and more. For example, they're now going on the same overseas exercises, and they're doing more exercises in common. On one, which is a patrol exercise in week 23, the girls take part in their own right. We're integrating them increasingly, although the girls' service is different in certain ways, because of the job specification they have to meet." (Training officer, Sandhurst)

The Women's Royal Army Corps officer college at Camberley became a wing of Sandhurst in 1984. Unlike the men's courses, the WSC contains both graduates and non-graduates working side by side. The graduates have the status of probationary 2nd Lieutenants, as they do on the SGC. Non-graduate women enter Sandhurst as officer cadets, like the men on the SMC.

"The reason the women grads and non-grads are mixed in together is quite simple – the girls that come here are much more mature than the men. They're very competitive, and they do well. Last term in the top 12 in the identifiable order of merit of everyone on the courses, six were girls.

"They do a slightly different course, because they don't do as much tactics as the men, or as much weapons training. They just do the submachine gun and the pistol. They actually do more service writing, clerical etc., to fit them for the jobs they're likely to do, the majority being assistant adjutants on leaving here." (Training officer Sandhurst)

The first five weeks of all the courses is basic training. Ages, experiences and backgrounds vary widely, but everyone is assumed to be at the same level of ignorance. This is the essential 'square-bashing' interlude, at the end of which comes the first of several milestones – Passing off the Square. SMC and SGC have differing syllabi even for this initial training.

The SGC worksheet for the five weeks includes two extended exercises: one near Sandhurst, and the other in Wales. The SMC concentrates on the basics, listed as skill at arms, fieldcraft, map reading, first aid, drill, and army organization. Despite the difference in emphasis, the first impact of Sandhurst is a culture shock that varies in intensity according to background. Until recently, many cadets felt the initial phase was a deliberate battering down of their individuality.

"The first two or three days, in retrospect, they took it fairly easy on us. I was on the Standard Military Course. It was down the medical centre for jabs etc. They have videos on how to clean your teeth properly, with Snoopy and Woodstock showing you how. Also it was a case of our Colour Sergeant saying, 'This is how you iron a shirt, and this is how you make a bed-block etc'. The NCO lives out, but always seems to be there, only seems to require about one hour's sleep a night.

"There are individual rooms. I think they do that so there's more to clean. Basically, they're out to piss you off, and they make no bones about it. In those first

Below: Officers at Sandhurst get a broad, basic knowledge of weaponry. They also gain experience of handling civil disobedience and riot.

weeks you're learning to march, and use your weapon at a very basic level.

"By about week three you fire the first rounds. For some people that's a big event. You have so much kit, including NBC (nuclear, biological and chemical warfare) stuff. You have to clean it, and fold it, and you're still not sure what it's all for. Inspection's every morning. Reveille officially was 6.30, but you'd have to get up a couple of hours before that, because the sheets and blankets off the bed you'd been sleeping in had to be made into a bed-block. Most people just slept in their sleeping bags. That stops after about the fourth week, but it hangs over you as a threat." (Keith Harvey, ex-Sandhurst, ex-Royal Artillery)

The age of SMC cadets varies from 18 to 29. Just

under 50 per cent are from fee-paying schools, 36 per cent are from non-fee-paying schools, and about 13 per cent are from Welbeck, the army's sixth-form college. There are also a few cadets from the ranks. These have been identified as having the requisite qualities, and encouraged to apply for commissions. They are usually already on the NCO ladder, most commonly with the rank of corporal.

"By and large if a regiment produces a chap, they don't go back to that regiment as an officer. That's a rough rule of thumb. It's now pretty common to have people commissioned from Sandhurst who have other-ranks experience." (Training officer)

The SMC intakes come in three times a year, in January, May and September, with an average strength of about 170 per intake. The 'bull' of initial training has been modified in recent years.

"The programme runs from eight in the morning to about ten o'clock at night. Now that sounds awfully severe, but actually it's not, because a lot of that work is preparation for the following day, and it's in their own time . . . Spending so much time preparing kit that you never got to sleep properly might have happened a few years back, but it's something the last General got a grip of. It was called the 'black economy'. What was happening was that the enthusiasm of the instructors was to try and be best at everything, and of course that put the cadets under unnecessary pressure." (Training officer)

Passing off the Square marks the transition from basic training to the beginning of officer training. From now on, apart from the special tactical training and the exercises geared to it, there will be a constant thread of regular classes in leadership, signals, skill at arms, field-craft, physical training and games. Drill also continues, but with a reduced number of periods.

Physical fitness is of paramount importance. For some, who were used to PE and games at school, the fitness programme will not be too bad. For others, reaching the required standards may become a major preoccupation and source of grief.

"The first thing they say is, 'We will progressively build up your fitness, so don't worry, gentlemen'. And then the first week, lesson one, you do three sit-ups, and lesson two you do 20, and then three days later you're expected to do 400, and that's the progression. But before you join, your joining instructions include a little pamphlet on the recommended level of fitness, and how to attain it, so most people have been out running before getting there.

"The first week you'll go out maybe three times for a half-hour run. By the middle of the course, which is

Above left: Sophisticated night-vision equipment being used to detect a target. Cadets on exercises have opportunities to use such equipment but they would also be concerned with the theory and practice of navigation and physical fitness exercises (left).

"Most people who join the army, and I'm talking in very general terms, want to climb a mountain, shoot a gun and sleep under the stars. So what we try and do is to give them that as soon as possible, and put them on a little exercise. If they didn't have it we'd have disappointed people, and disappointed people wouldn't stay here. The graduates carry out Exercise First Flush at Pippingford Park, a local training area.

"It's a 'round robin', with a little bit of leadership, and quite a lot of cross-country movement and navigation. They're in groups, and someone is appointed in charge of each group. In the navigation there's a degree of fitness involved, because they have to go against the clock from A to B. At each stand they do a task. It can be a purely command task, a 60-gallon (270-l) drum, a plank that's too short and a piece of string that won't reach – that sort of thing, or it could be something more pertinent to training, such as a map-reading question.

"It comes very early, but don't forget that quite a lot of the graduates have been to university OTC, which makes a big difference. All told they do about 36 hours' worth and they sleep out in bivouacs. They have to be taught how to do it, so it doesn't come as too much of a shock, and they've got the right kit, sleeping bags, ration packs . . . we're not trying to destroy them." (Training officer)

The SMC does a similar exercise later in their course. The non-graduates have a one-day Self Reliance exercise in week seven. In week nine their tactical training begins, and they have their first 36-hour exercise the same week. In the following four weeks, tactical training is concentrated on patrols and battle drills at section and platoon level. Exercise Switch Back in week 11 lasts two days, with patrols and section battle drills. Exercise Sarum Steppe, held on Salisbury Plain over three days in week 12, adds platoon battle drills. In the same week the cadets take Military Knowledge Test 1 (MK1). This contains questions on subjects such as tactics, first aid, map reading, and army structures. MK2 is in week 26, and MK3 in week 39.

Exercise Hat Trick lasts 36 hours and is in week 13. As the exercises progress, the tasks involved in them increase in complexity, bringing in new elements from the training classes as they are covered. Signals and map reading cease to be academic subjects and become 'hands-on'. On exercise the teams have to navigate, and use grid references, using the correct procedures to send them where necessary over the radio, and combining these technical tasks with the strenuous and precise work of the battle drills.

At the end of the term there are competitions to decide the Sovereign's Platoon, including drill, orienteering, steeple-chase and march-and-shoot. All first

when most people are at their fittest, you're going for maybe an hour and a half run with all your kit on. You start off with skeleton webbing, just basic, then you add more and more pouches, and it gets heavier and heavier. The fitness side is quite well done." (Keith Harvey, ex-Sandhurst, ex-Royal Artillery)

Probationers entering the SGC are on average aged about 23. About 65 per cent come from non-fee-paying schools, and the rest from fee-paying schools. At least 15 per cent have degrees from Oxford or Cambridge, 73 per cent have degrees from other universities and 12 per cent have graduated from polytechnics. The SGC intakes are in January and September. The January intake is the smaller, at up to 100 entrants. The September intake, which ties in with the end of most university courses, is of about 270. In week two the SGC members take part in Exercise First Flush.

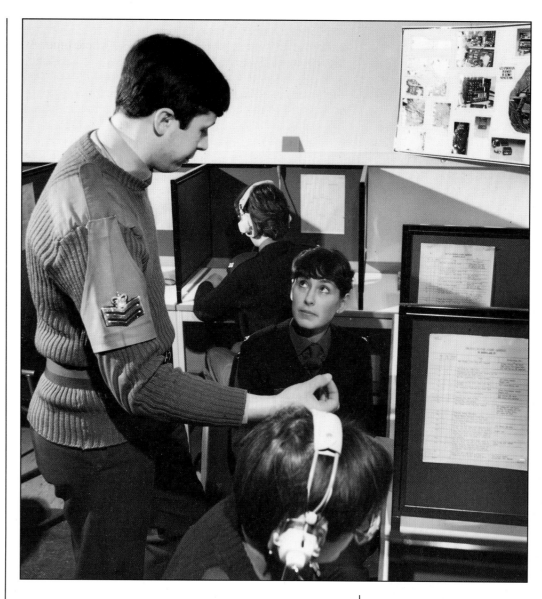

Left: A training session at Sandhurst, where extensive use is made of audio-visual aids. Once cadets have 'passed off the square', officer training takes the form of regular classes in subjects such as signals, leadership, fieldcraft and skill at arms, with progressively less emphasis on drill.

termers, graduates and non-graduates, take part in the Sovereign's Parade which marks the passing-out of Sandhurst of the senior intakes.

At least a week of the leave which separates the first from the second term must be taken up in 'adventurous activities'. A favourite option is a Unit Expedition Leaders' course in Wales. It is also possible to participate in parachuting and flying courses, those who complete the flying course qualifying for their private pilot's licence.

In the second term the tactics lessons and exercises continue to run parallel with the programme of basic instructions. But now the interest is heightened by a number of new elements. In week 19 the SMC begins the NBC warfare classes which the SGC had already started seven weeks earlier. Week 21 marks the end of the Conventional Warfare phase, and the beginning of the Counter Revolutionary Warfare (CRW) phase of training. CRW exercises are popular, as they closely simulate real conditions and confrontations.

"The CRW exercise can actually get the adrenalin going, because there are certain bits of crowd control,

Right: Women on the Women's Standard Course (WSC) at Sandhurst, where nongraduates and graduates work together.

riot control, practised in it. That's always enjoyable." (Training officer)

CRW training is carried out in urban and in rural environments, together with the practice of more general Internal Security (IS) techniques such as car searches. Regular soldiers are willing 'enemy' for the exercises. Clad in visored helmets and wielding riot shields and truncheons, the cadets have a taste of riot control, coming under a barrage of half bricks and other missiles as well as provocative abuse. Those that go on with their regiments to Northern Ireland will probably receive further specialist training, but the Sandhurst IS experience is a useful introduction to the sound and feel of violence and confrontation.

Throughout all the exercises, classes, and even the huge range of sports and recreations that RMAS facilitates, runs the theme of leadership and assessment. "The whole raison d'être of Sandhurst is leadership training. We're not here to turn out an infantry officer, a gunner officer, a cavalry officer – we're here to turn out a basic officer who then goes on to an arms school and then becomes a specialist. Our aim is to produce leaders. We've taken out the academic content which existed when I was here as a cadet – I did the two-year course. The first term was mainly military, then I did four terms of mainly academically orientated training, then the last term was military again. Since the Mons establishment, which was set up really to cater for

Short Service Commission officers, moved to Sandhurst, we have a mixture of three-year and longer engagement cadets. It would be ludicrous to invest two years of someone's time in basic officer training if they're only going to be in the army for three years. "All the sport played here has a tremendous spin-off. A young officer leaving here who's competent in sport can take his platoon or his troop straight away. It's a tremendous tool in leadership. The Communication Skills part of the course is also a very important part of leadership. If you can't communicate with your soldiers, you're not going to be much good. The Communications Department has been in existence since 1986. They use TV and video equipment and techniques as part of the learning process. SMC now has some 59 hours of communications training, and the graduates and the

girls have about 20 hours.

"The assessment process goes on the whole time. At platoon level the Platoon Commander, who is a captain, and the Platoon Colour Sergeant continually discuss their cadets. The captains are specifically chosen to come to Sandhurst, and the Colour Sergeants undergo a five-week test before they are let loose on the cadets.

"The cadets are also assessed by the Company Commander and by the College Commander, who is a full colonel. And, of course, the Commandant reviews all these assessments. Each term there is a Progress Board. This is held by the College Commander, and prior to that the notes and files on each chap are brought up to date. There's also an input from the PT Wing, as well as the Signals Wing and the Skill at Arms Wing. So it's a very broad assessment. We're looking for strengths as well as weaknesses. The Commandant also gets together with the College Commander to review the cases of the weaker brethren, to consider whether they should continue training or not. The overall wastage rate is about 10 per cent, representing 6.5 per cent for the SMC, 12 per cent for the SGC and 4 per cent for the WSC." (Lt Colonel D A H Green SO1 G3 (Trg.))

The traditional 'gentleman cadet' image still persists at Sandhurst. Along with the rugby, cricket, hockey and soccer, there are cadet-organized pastimes such as beagling, drag-hunting, game-shooting and fishing. Riding is no longer a compulsory skill. Some gentlemanly accomplishments are still on the syllabus.

"On the social side they're taught formal mess behaviour, the courtesies and etiquette required in an officers' mess, the procedure at regimental guest nights, and so forth. There's only one way to teach something like that, and that's to have one. Each Company has a guest night each term, and they invite Staff Officers, the Commandant, and some outside people." (Training officer)

Some things are not taught formally, but absorbed by keeping a wary eye out for one's more elegant and socially assured peers.

"We all turned up with our suitcases, and our suits on, and all the wrong shoes, and unacceptable white socks. There were about 180 of us. There were some rankers. We had a corporal from REME. Initially, they really go for this officer image – the correct jacket, the correct haircut, the correct way of speaking, everything about them. Everyone, all the seniors, look the part. It's quite intimidating. But apart from the really self-assured Eton types everyone of the new boys is thinking, 'My God, they all look like officers, and I don't know what I'm doing here!' You soon learn what's an unacceptable jacket and an unacceptable shoe. Basically, they're looking for money in the clothing. None of my stuff looked elegant or expensive enough." (Ex-SMC cadet)

In week 23 the SGC and the WSC do their joint exercise, which is All Arms, and mechanized. In weeks 27/28 the SGC does its Threshold exercise. This is the

Rowallan Company

In 1977 Rowallan Company was set up at Sandhurst at the instigation of the Regular Commissions Board, which is the main filtering organization for those hoping to attend the academy. In assessing would-be cadets, there was often a 'grey' area of candidates who did not meet the Board's requirements, but who might, with some encouragement, be drawn out to a level of maturity and of self-confidence which could help them to have a successful career in the army and so benefit themselves and the army.

Rowallan Company's main purpose was to instil, through a rigorous and challenging physical programme, a sound foundation for leadership qualities. In World War II, Lord Rowallan had run an arduous Highland Fieldcraft Training Centre in Scotland, under the maxim, 'Develop character first and military leadership will follow'. The 12-week Rowallan course resembles nothing so much as concentrated training for special forces. Unlike those on the commissioning courses those accepted into Rowallan Company are private soldiers and are treated as such. They are in the army, draw a private's pay, eat in the soldiers' dining hall, and sleep in barrack accommodation.

The basic principle of the course is to punish failure and reward success. The emphasis is away from formal military training, and towards physical fitness, self-reliance, and communications skills. There are three major exercises dividing the course into four phases of three weeks each. With the benefit of an unusually high staff-to-student ratio, the Rowallan cadets work through a punishing and exhilarating programme which embraces self-reliance skills, such as rock-climbing, abseiling, cross-country navigation, outdoor survival techniques, first aid, kayaking, rescue work and mountaineering. As skills and fitness mount, they are brought increasingly into play in team situations, so that leadership qualities can be identified, encouraged and given the opportunity to flourish.

The rigours of the Rowallan course take their toll of candidates. Sometimes more than a third do not complete the course, either opting out or else being eliminated by the staff. However, of those that pass out successfully, to go on to the SMC, there is a high proportion of above-average achievers. They are extremely fit and self-confident, and can operate positively in team situations, and take initiatives. Compared with other SMC cadets, more ex-Rowallan men pass out of Sandhurst above average, a greater percentage get average marks, and fewer get back-termed or fail. They have been known to say that after Rowallan they can handle anything that's thrown at them by the army or any other establishment they are likely to encounter.

Above: Keith Harvey (left) and colleagues on specialist duties. He graduated from Sandhurst and found it a worthwhile challenge.

most major undertaking of the entire course, and the culminating testing ground for the months of training and learning. Threshold always takes place overseas, usually in Cyprus or West Germany, but sometimes in France. This is a full-blown combat exercise with a complex series of scenarios and full logistical back-up.

The SMC has its own Threshold exercise in week 36. Both SGC and SMC finish their Sandhurst apprenticeships with the formal ceremony of the Sovereign's Parade, and the Commissioning Ball hosted by each departing senior intake. On the Parade the cadets wear their Sandhurst Number Ones, and then at the ball that night they get to wear their regimental mess kit for the first time.

"Some people are interviewed at the regiment of their choice before going to Sandhurst. Some people's fathers and grandfathers have been in the Guards, and that's where they are going. I was one of those who were late in choosing. You wear no regimental insignia until the final attack of the final exercise, which for me

get maybe three weeks, then you do another period of 'special to arm' training. In the Artillery, which I had opted for, you go down to the big artillery school at Larkhill. After that I went on to join 50 Missile Regiment, at Menden in the Ruhr Valley, where I was in charge of a Lance missile team.

"Someone said that someone who hasn't ever been a soldier always has a part of him that regrets it. I think that's true." (Keith Harvey)

France's ESM

The land-based forces of the French Army train practically all their regular officers at the École Spéciale Militaire de Saint-Cyr, known as the ESM. Set up originally by Napoleon Bonaparte in 1802, the school was installed two years later at the Palace of Fontaine-bleau. In 1808 it moved to the old royal palace of St Louis at Saint-Cyr, close to Paris. The 655 pupils took three days to march there, accompanied by drums, and the school remained at the same site until after World War II.

During the German Occupation 'Free-French Saint-Cyr' continued to operate in exile in Algeria and Britain. Allied bombing destroyed the old buildings in 1944. After the war the school was reopened in Brittany on a 20-square mile (52-km^2) site at Coëtquidan, 28 miles (45 km) south-west of Rennes.

There are currently three main officer training establishments at the Coëtquidan complex. The École Spéciale Militaire de Saint-Cyr is the major training school for aspiring regular officers entering by competitive examination. The École Militaire Interarmes (EMIA) is the school which prepares serving NCOs for commissions. Also at Coëtquidan is the École Militaire du Corps Technique et Administratif (EMCTA) for entrants to technical and administrative branches both from the ranks and from civilian life.

Men on the ESM, the main source of regular officers, are known as candidates rather than cadets, which is associated with the military structures of the pre-Revolutionary *ancien régime*.

In 1982 the school's course was extended from two to three years, and the following year it received its first two female candidates. ESM entrants can sit one of five competitive examinations to gain a place on the three-year course: a science exam for those with high-grade mathematical qualifications; a literature and humanities exam for literature students; an economics exam for primary economics students; an exam for those with a good secondary education diploma; and an exam for candidates from certain engineering schools. All candidates have to be under the age of 22 on January 1st of the year they take the exam. Candidates already in the services, or who have completed National Service, can be a year older.

Before signing on the dotted line, all candidates have to undergo a medical test. Any doubtful cases are referred to an army specialist, who passes the word

was the climax of the whole course, when everyone traditionally put on the beret with the cap-badge of the regiment they were going to.

"In your final term at Sandhurst, as the Senior Division, the Colour Sergeant actually talks to you as well as gives you orders, but the gap always remains between cadets and instructors. You do find that you can get away with more. In fact, I think you're almost expected to bend rules, just getting in in the nick of time before a parade, and so on. If you don't, then they worry about you. When my regiment was in Germany, we had some American officers with us, and some of them were West Pointers. Their officer training ethos was that if anyone stepped out of line, they not only told him he was doing so, but also informed on him 'for the integrity of the officer corps'. They've got a very different attitude. At Sandhurst it's very much the unwritten rule that you never snitch on anyone.

"Personally, Sandhurst was an adventure for me. I had always been intrigued by the idea of officer training, Sandhurst in particular. It was that feeling that 'I really want to have a hard time and do things that few people do' – just like the adverts. I was determined to enjoy myself and soak it all up. At the end of Sandhurst you down: fit for service, unfit for service, or 'come back in a year's time'.

The ESM's year begins in September and ends in August, the inviolable French month of rest and holiday. In that first year the bulk of the purely military instruction is achieved, with an accompanying strand of physical fitness training and sport. As at Sandhurst and West Point, sport is pursued with an almost obsessive enthusiasm. Rugby is the main sport, but there is a wide range of other options, including soccer, volleyball and athletics. Each year Saint-Cyr takes part in a 'taiam', an athletic meet involving officer-cadet establishments from several European countries, including The Netherlands, Britain and West Germany.

Between January and June inclusive, the pupils spend five months with a regimental unit of their prospective branch, getting experience as section commanders over trainee soldiers. This is followed by a month at the National Commando Training Centre, again as section commanders over trainees.

In the second academic year, basic military instruction takes a back-seat to general education, embracing a wide spectrum of disciplines and subjects. The technical subjects covered include shooting, transport, radio, anti-aircraft combat, NBC, engineering and information. At the end of June the high-point, literally, is qualifying for a military parachutist's certificate. By the end of ESM training, each candidate will have carried out at least six parachute jumps. They also qualify as lifeguards, with a national life-saving certificate.

In the third year of the ESM, the students are now 2nd Lieutenants. The General Education component of the year's work includes an emphasis on language training – particularly English, as well as an analysis of contemporary history and economics.

On the physical side, the pupils receive horse-riding training, practice hand-to-hand combat, learn how to teach PT, and qualify for a diploma in the organization of a chosen sporting speciality.

On the military side, they gain experience of military co-operation with other branches of the armed forces, and, if possible, are given experience of active service in an overseas theatre, in a unit of their chosen branch.

Despite the modern subjects of the syllabus, and the modern military skills, the three-year ESM course has a strong traditional element. Three years is sufficient time to be expansive, and traditional celebrations include a spectacular annual recreation of the Battle of Austerlitz, and the hosting of a number of formal visits, including the 'corniches', who are the pre-Saint-Cyr students undergoing their two-year preparatory period. The third-year Saint-Cyriens constitute the Premier French Battalion. They lead the parade and meet the President during the July 14th celebrations in the Champs Élysées, and pass out of the École Spéciale Militaire de Saint-Cyr in the impressive parade known as a Triomphe.

All officers, on completing their commissioning courses,

Above: Officer training at Saint-Cyr is a combination of arduous exercises to develop physical fitness, and concerted academic and military studies.

must go on to complete a further year at the trade-school – école d'application – relevant to their chosen branch of the army. These are: infantry – Montpellier; armour and cavalry – Saumur; artillery – Draguignan; engineers – Angers; signals – Montargis; transport – Tours; logistics service – Bourges; Gendarmerie – Melun; and aviation – Le Luc.

US officer training

On January 20 1989, when the newly inaugurated President Bush of the USA took to the reviewing stand near the White House, the first of the 211 military units to march down Pennsylvania Avenue to salute their new chief were the cadets of the US Military Academy at West Point, NY. Like their brothers in arms at the École Spéciale Militaire de Saint-Cyr in France, the West Pointers are their nation's most senior unit, and it was unthinkable that any other military group should head the inaugural parade.

West Pointers are sticklers for traditional form, as befits the members of an organization set up in 1802 and attended by some of the most illustrious names in American military and political history. West Point's site, on the west bank of the Hudson River has been continuously occupied by the military since 1778.

Following the Revolutionary War, General Washington was acutely aware that victory had been owed in considerable measure to the expertise provided by professional European soldiers. Americans generally mistrusted the idea of a professional army, and the House of Representatives did not adopt a resolution favouring the establishment of an academy until the end of 1801. The first classes were held in April 1802. Throughout its history West Point has been a scientific academy, with the emphasis mostly on engineering – the key military science of the last two centuries.

Today's West Point provides its cadets with a four-year academic curriculum which culminates in the award of a Bachelor of Science degree. Entry to the academy is via academic qualification, rigorous testing, and official nomination by senators, congressmen, the President and Vice-President, and various institutions. All these sources of nomination have fixed allotments of places at West Point. The authorized strength of the academy is more than 2,500, and competition for nominations and places is fierce, as West Point is the main source of Regular officers. And in the field of promotion in the higher echelons of the army, to be a member of the West Point old boys' network is still

Below: The third-year Saint-Cyriens are the Premier French Battalion. They lead the July 14th celebrations and pass out in the impressive Triomphe parade.

considered by many to be a distinct advantage.

Unlike Sandhurst, with its short courses and minimal academic orientation, or Saint-Cyr, with its strong emphasis on a wide-ranging military instruction, West Point does not provide much 'hands-on' military experience. The academy is run with military discipline, and the cadets spend all their working hours in uniform, yet the emphasis remains academic. And in the early years of an officer's career, to have been at West Point confers no practical advantages.

Most of the officers in the US Army enter the service and their commissions by other routes, chiefly the Reserve Officers Training Corps (ROTC), which is administered by TRADOC, the army's training arm via some 250 colleges and universities. Students carry out a limited military training syllabus alongside their ordinary studies. On graduation they receive commissions if they are considered suitable, and have to pledge a minimum period of active duty if they take them up. Enlisted men are prepared for commissions through Officer Candidate Schools.

The US Army is today probably the most training-conscious army in the world, and provides a vast array of training programmes and facilities for enlisted men and officers alike. As well as the most up-to-date combat-simulation training programmes provided by the new Combat Training Centers, such as the National Training Center at Fort Irwin, California, and the Combat Maneuver Training Center at Hohenfels, West Germany, the army provides retraining schools that enable officers and men to change course, often several times in a career. The process is seen as cumulative. With each new orientation, the officer adds a string to his bow, enabling him to be called on in a widening range of roles. This flexibility, particularly of the officer corps, is seen as ample justification for the considerable expense of the constantly updated training programmes.

Lt Col D L Prins

Lieutenant-Colonel D L Prins' case is a good example of the constant-training pattern that is followed by modern army officers. In effect, training never ceases, even at relatively high rank. In the course of a 22-year army career, Lt Col Prins has worn a number of hats.

"I started off going through university – West Michigan, in Kalamazoo, Michigan, and took the ROTC training while I was there, though initially I had no intentions of ever going in the army. However, it was during the Vietnam time-frame, and I realised I had the option of going in as a draftee or going in as an officer, so I decided to stick in the ROTC programme.

"At the end of my junior year they asked for volunteers to go to flight school. I volunteered, passed the medical and the written exam, and in my senior year in university they sent me to the local airport to acquire my civilian private pilot's licence, training in the Cessna 150.

"On graduation I went straight into the army, already

with a little bit of flying experience under my belt. I went in initially as an infantry officer, and did my basic Officer Training Course at Fort Benning, Georgia. That was six weeks. Then I went straight to flight school, which is a nine-month course. I was still a 2nd lieutenant at this point. The first four months of flight school were at Fort Wolters, Texas, about a two-hour drive west of Dallas. We flew half the day, and had academic training half the day. I was training for helicopter pilot.

"We started off in the Hiller OH-23 – that's the old plastic-bubble training plane, six-cylinder gasoline engine. So old it's not on the inventory any longer. It was old then, in 1968/69. We left Fort Wolters after four months, and I went on to Savannah, Georgia.

"We had about 100 flight hours and were still not

pilots as far as the army was concerned. We could fly straight and level in nice sunny weather, but couldn't do anything special yet. At Savannah we began instrument training, in the OH-13 'T' Model. For about 40 hours we did nothing but instrument work. They put the visors on you and you do all your flying strictly by the instruments.

"After that we transferred to the UH-1, the 'Huey', and did another 50 hours in that, and then we graduated. We were now Army Aviators, with our wings on our chests. The entire time we'd been doing four hours academics a day and four hours on the flight line. Pilot is not necessarily a commissioned rank. We also had Warrant Officer aviators.

"The WO's job for the rest of their career is to fly. The commissioned officer will be a platoon leader, company commander, battalion commander, and then he'll rotate to a staff job where he may not fly at all. Then he may rotate back into flying.

"The academic stuff was all aviation-related – what makes a helicopter fly, etc. We also learned how to call for artillery and air strikes. Toward the end we did air-lifting of soldiers under an instructor-pilot, working with infantrymen also under training.

"Then I did a year at Fort McClellan, Alabama with an aviation detachment, flying OH-13s and Hueys on training missions. We ferried troops from A to B, did insertions and other wargames, working single-aircraft, multi-aircraft, gaining pilot skills as well as working in fire teams. Then we went to Vietnam.

"I was assigned to a reconnaissance unit. I flew the scout aircraft, the OH-6. We worked in teams of two – one OH-6 and one Cobra gunship. The Cobra would fly about 1,000 ft above ground level, in big lazy circles, and the OH-6 would fly tree-top, looking for whatever he could find, following trails, flying over jungle and open country, just looking.

"We used to call it Reconnaissance with Sacrifice, because the little guy usually got shot at, drew fire, then the Cobra could roll in and try to even the sides. I was in Vietnam for one year, long enough to get shot down a couple of times. I wasn't badly injured, a little bit of shrapnel. You learned how to crash-land in the trees, then your team came and got you fast. I've seen other aircraft come in and get shot down in the same place trying to rescue the down-crew.

"From Vietnam I went to Fort Hood, Texas, and was with the First Cavalry Division there, experimenting with what they called the tri-capability division – Tricap. They had a brigade of infantry, a brigade of armour and a brigade of aviation. We experimented using the helicopter in the anti-tank role, which is what the current thing is today. This was continuous training, learning something new every day. We learned in Vietnam you could fly high and be safe, or you could fly

Left: West Point cadets get a minimal amount of military instruction. The four-year course is essentially academic, leading to a science degree.

tree-top and be safe. But then we said, OK, now if we go to the European theatre and fly, the surface-to-air missiles are going to eat your lunch. At the end of the Vietnam War they began to use the shoulder-fired Grail missiles, the heat-seekers, and your turbine engines put out about 600°C exhaust, which is a good target.

"So at Fort Hood we did nothing but low-level flying, called Nap of the Earth (NOE) and we did the initial experimentation with the helicopter gunship in the anti-tank role. We did exercises, demonstrations, two-, three- and four-week wargame scenarios against armoured divisions, with all kinds of VIPs coming through to see how it worked.

"At Fort Hood I became a company commander, and then went into a staff position where I ran a Cobra transition course for regular army pilots, transitioning them from Hueys to Cobras, about 20 a month.

"From there I went to Fort Knox, Kentucky to the Armor Officer Advanced Course, six months, strictly academic, on everything from how to run an orderly room to how to fight the new ambush defence tactics, primarily in the armour mode. There were about 300 captains on that course, some of us pilots, but the majority straight tankers. We also did NBC stuff, engineering, demolition. We had about three practicals out in the field, playing wargames against each other.

"From there I went to Recruiting Command in Cleveland, Ohio, and was given an area, recruiting male and female soldiers into the army – I had 18 sergeants to help me. When I went through the ROTC programme as a student there were no females in it. Now there's a lot of females going through ROTC and West Point. There are female pilots, too, primarily in the maintenance end of it. We still have the rules that a woman will not be put in a position where she would be expected to fight. Maybe 8 per cent of pilots are now female, but not in the infantry, the armour or the artillery.

"After Recruiting Command I went to Presidio, San Francisco. While I was there I worked on my own time to take the Commander General Staff College course. Some get selected for a six-month course at Fort Leavenworth. I took it by correspondence. It took three years, doing it the hard way, while working for the army full-time during the day. Then I was promoted to Lieutenant Colonel.

"That was my last academic thing. Everything else has been on-the-job training – OJT we call it. I'll have 22 years in by July this year. I'm 43 years old, and I've got some 2,100 hours of flying as an Army Aviator."

Chapter 8

FORCES DIARY:
Review of the year

As we enter the last decade of what must surely be considered the most extraordinary century in the history of mankind, Forces Diary reviews the events of 1989 in their military and political context. Concentrating on the momentous activities that have so recently shaken and stirred the East/West cocktail, the review also looks at prevailing trends and strategies for NATO, the UN, Europe, Central Africa, and the Middle East.

A demonstration in the Middle East. About 130,000 lives have been lost in and around Beirut since 1975, when the Syrians and Israelis became involved. Last year the street fighting, shelling and indiscriminate murder reached a peak of mad violence.

The start of a new decade, like the start of a new year, is always a time when people of all cultures and with all kinds of political and ideological differences make noises about change for the better, either to strengthen their own positions or to link hands and try to absorb culturally rooted differences in a more friendly fashion. Such cathartic behaviour is particularly poignant in the last decade of the 20th century after the best part of 100 years in which humans have, according to historians, let more blood and created more life-manacling environmental mess than in the whole of the previous evolution of the species.

The year 1989 offered certain important anniversaries. On September 3 1989, the 50th anniversary of the commencement of World War II was remembered with public and private awe and a ceremony of rekindled grief. So much was – and remains – unknown about those exceptional years. Like the trauma in human memory that they represent, fact and fiction combine in the steady unveiling of the events that relate to the War and which continue to erupt in its wake. Of the many new or revivifying publications about the War which came out last year, *War Wives* (1989) by Eileen and Colin Townsend offered an interesting perspective.

The book is about the women in Germany and Britain who were left behind. Although the terrible dangers that their menfolk confronted were made more tolerable in some ways by the enlargement of horizons, or by the chances of glory they may have experienced, the book describes the drabness, separation and danger experienced by their wives. Perhaps fittingly, it is a German woman who writes: 'Even today, when I see pictures on television of how things were, I feel ill. Please God, let there never be another war'.

What were you thinking at 11am on Sunday September 3rd last? Extraordinarily, with new, radically different generations growing up and with only a tiny proportion of the population having experienced life-committing deeds in action (even among those in the Armed Forces), there are still some people who will discreetly admit that they would actually enjoy a war, because to be in constant danger of one's life is to be most alive. But the machinery of war today forbids war in this sense, except in small and usually inglorious pockets of the globe or in the grey areas of foreign interactions.

Largely unknown to the public in Britain, since World War II, the British Armed Forces have been on active service about 100 times, including The Falklands Campaign and not including many repeated periods of active service shared between various Army Regiments and the Royal Marines in Northern Ireland.

NATO's birthday

Life begins at 40, or so some people in Brussels may hope, for the North Atlantic Treaty Organization (NATO) which, without too much fanfare, celebrated 40 years on April 4 1989 since its formal establishment. Parades in the snow marked the occasion, together with warnings that NATO plans to live on for at least another four decades, whatever the social, economic and military reforms achieved by Moscow and Eastern Europe. The Secretary General of NATO, Manfred Worner, received most press attention at the occasion and while a relatively unexcited crowd ferreted through make-shift souvenir stalls to find and purchase 40-year mementoes, he told the ambassadors of the 16-member nations of the Alliance that they 'remained the backbone and lighthouse of mankind's future in freedom and peace'. He went on to defend NATO's policy of nuclear deterrence as the 'bedrock of our security'.

Manfred Worner is very much the mouthpiece of the faction in Brussels that believes the West should not be seduced into thinking that the Warsaw Pact no longer poses a threat. NATO should, he argued, 'make a careful distinction between the short-term, peaceful aims of Mikhail Gorbachev and the enduring long-term potential of the Soviet Union as a geo-political power. Mr Gorbachev is trying to reform his own society and economy and he does not want to engage in a war, not least because of NATO. But the potential – the capability – is still underestimated. Looking at the potential, there is still risk . . . There are risks of a historical period of transition which you have to calculate. NATO must stay as the framework of security and stability while the Soviet Union will remain, for geo-political reasons, a dominant factor.'

These and other comments beg important questions. More people last year, rightly or wrongly, began to think of Mikhail Gorbachev as an international benefactor rather more than a cold-war bear, and when such a notion becomes popular, as Gorbachev has helped to ensure that it has, those concerned with the European

Left: Desolation and hopelessness in the city of Beirut, The Lebanon. Few people know exactly who is fighting whom and for what reason.

that the Soviet Union 'genuinely wants world peace' rose from just 6 per cent to 37 per cent.

Nevertheless, it appears that those in Brussels who wish to continue to justify NATO's policies need not worry too much. Nearly half of those interviewed in the poll were in favour of the continued presence of 330,000 American troops in Europe, viewing them as an important contribution to the security of Western Europe. Furthermore, there is a continued support for an independent nuclear deterrent although 76 per cent of those questioned thought that Europe would be safer (37 per cent), or as safe (39 per cent), if all nuclear weapons on both sides of the divide were abolished by the year 2000.

Shooting your own foot

Another interesting, although unsurprising factor, in the findings of the poll, was that it showed little comfort for those in favour of staunch unilateralism. Only a third of those questioned wanted to get rid of our independent deterrent, compared with 35 per cent who agreed there should be a reduction and 23 per cent who thought no change was necessary. In Britain, those of the soft left argued strongly that there should be a time limit imposed on any negotiations that may take place were the Labour Party to get into power, and added that it would be Labour's objective to rid Britain of its nuclear deterrent within the five-year period of its parliament.

Wrangling continues, with opponents to this 'soft' approach saying that there is little point in negotiating with such a definite aim in mind if the Soviet Union were fully aware that the Labour Government would give up British nuclear weapons in five years time anyway. There is little doubt that this counter argument is right. If the cold war period has proved anything, apart from the effectiveness and necessary evil of dirty tricks in

Below: Germany 50 years ago – a scene of human tragedy, showing hungry Germans rummaging through the carriages of their own train to find food and clothing.

front line have to work much harder to convince their tax-paying electorates that what they stand for and are doing is relevant and right. All but a tiny minority, would wish to see a disbandment or weakening of NATO, even with a stronger growth of feeling of Europeanism.

It is unsettling that NATO chiefs continue to portray the Soviet Union in a devilish image, apparently to justify European forward defence policies. These policies need not be apologised for. The leadership of the Soviet Union would not hold its European neighbours in much respect if they were to down the barriers or drop arms in expectation of embrace when the Warsaw Pact's conventional arsenal, chemical weapons capability and defence spending continue to outstrip Europe's equivalent by a wide margin.

Public opinion regarding the Soviet Union has certainly changed. Last year, for the third time in the last decade, Britain's *The Times*, supported by the Council of Defence Information, published a MORI poll which endeavoured to gauge public perceptions about the Superpowers and how these perceptions changed in the 1980s.

The poll indicated that in 1981, 70 per cent of respondents, aged 15 plus, reckoned that the Soviet Union 'wished to extend its powers over other countries', compared with 31 per cent who selected the USA; in 1983, the figures were 59 per cent for the USSR and 26 per cent for the USA; and in 1989, they were 35 per cent, USSR, 33 per cent, USA.

Other questions indicated the softening of British perceptions about the USSR. For example, only 17 per cent of 2,025 respondents in 1989 believed that Soviet policies are harmful to Britain, compared with 42 per cent in 1981. In this period, the number who believe international politics, it must be that to defend yourself effectively is to demonstrate an offensive capability from, if possible, a position of strength. We all learn this in the playground.

Short-range weapon modernization

In the event of Gorbachev's visit to the West last year, many worries and arguments between rival factions in NATO were exacerbated. In particular Britain and the USA were put under pressure to slacken their firm position on the modernization of short-range nuclear missiles in Europe. The principal bone of contention is the modernization of the ageing tactical warhead Lance missiles, particularly between the Anglo-American and West German factions.

Appearing to support Bonn, the Belgian Prime Minister, Mr Wilfried Martens, has warned the Alliance that his coalition government would not support any decision on modernizing Lance before 1991-92 – the timetable favoured by London and Washington. Mr Martens did not disfavour an upgrading of Lance but insisted that any such system should not have a significantly increased range.

On the other hand, General John Galvin, NATO's Supreme Allied Commander, together with the British, wants a new weapons system with a range of about 280 miles (450 km) rather than the existing 70-mile (113-km) range. Mr Martens was also firm in wanting negotiations on the reduction of short-range nuclear weapons to take place as soon as possible and in this West Germany, Denmark and Greece all agreed.

At the same time, seven member nations of the Warsaw Pact launched a salvo demanding that talks about short-range weapons take place as quickly as possible with the aim of totally eliminating them from Europe along with intermediate-range weapons under the protocols of the INF treaty of May and October 1988. This, the so called 'Third Zero' option, is opposed by a consensus of NATO ministers. The row over Lance modernization, which has in fact been brewing for a number of years, dominated the 1989 NATO summit in May, the outcome of which was a directive drawn up to ensure a programme of modernization to commence in 1992 (or, by implication, thereabouts) with oblique reference only to the revamped weapons' projected range and capability.

Strongly opposing the views of the Bonn Government and the vociferous Belgians, Britain's then foreign minister, Sir Geoffrey Howe, gave a speech to the Royal United Services Institute in which he warned his West European counterparts not to go soft. He said that there was a shared interest in reducing strategic arms and nuclear weapons but as regards the European arsenal, the aim of Western governments was to maintain nuclear deterrence while that of the Soviet Union was the de-nuclearization of Europe.

For their part, reported Howe, some representatives of the Federal Republic were already looking to dispose of a forward defence in Europe. Commented Howe: 'We do not do ourselves a service by allowing the illusion to spread . . . that political and military changes which we hope one day will happen, have happened already . . .' Sir Geoffrey Howe, and other 'hard' leaders in NATO, reckon that any propaganda points achieved by the Soviets over the potentially extended range of the Lance missiles could easily be countered by the fact that despite the total ban on all intermediate-range weapons – 310-3,100 miles (500 km-5,000 km) – the Soviet's strategic nuclear arsenal (long range) is well capable of being trajectoried towards Europe.

Other factors could be added to this argument. At the beginning of the last decade, in 1980, NATO and Warsaw Pact tactical missiles numbered roughly the same. Since then, the Soviets have 'modernized' their missiles and now have approximately 12 times as many as there are on the NATO side. The modernization of Lance missiles would appear to be a prerequisite for ensuring East-West stability even if the exact replacement system is not specified for another two years. Last year Britain undertook to take six more long-range US F-111 bombers into its UK bases and thereby helped to offset West Germany's fear of carrying the greater deployment burden of NATO's nuclear arsenal.

The USA and Europe

With the Bush administration folding back its first calendar year, the US position in NATO is increasingly being questioned. As 1992 approaches – the date when the European Economic Community becomes a united, free market – the British are increasingly being asked to see themselves as European. Even the French (who more conspicuously occupy that part of the Western continental shelf) are beginning to think European and,

Left: Artillerymen from 50 Missile Regiment, Royal Artillery, stationed in West Germany, train with a Lance missile – part of NATO's armoury.

Above: An F-111C taxiing – a variant of the supersonic strike/attack aircraft, stationed in Britain, that President Reagan ordered to make strikes on Libya.

with the establishment of the small Franco-German Brigade, are looking for partners in security for the first time in a long while. But for Fortress Europe to become a reality in both military and economic terms, there are many questions to ponder regarding US involvement.

For example, unless the USA withdraws its 330,000 troops completely (which is currently unthinkable) or partly (but by what amount?) how can Europeans see themselves as a singular defensive entity? Another question: when the Americans, in an attempt to put pay to the long-standing problem of the budget deficit (currently still running high enough to instill speculative caution and concern in various global economic markets) decide at congressional level to ask the European members to pay a higher share towards the NATO Armed Forces bill, does this mean that the USA wants to pay less themselves, or does it mean that they wish Europe merely to catch up and take on greater responsibility?

Two factions in congress are already making themselves heard over this question. One view is that the Americans should do less, leaving the Europeans to do more. The other is that the Americans should do less so that the Alliance can concentrate less on nuclear weapons.

In the European forum, the question of the degree of US involvement in Europe poses head-scratchers all around. For example, in the burden-sharing equation, which nations in Europe foot what bill and how do they decide when certain nations' strategic interests do not necessarily relate to their capability to pay as much as others? Would the British feel happy about recruiting and maintaining more troops for the British Army of the Rhine when Britain's biggest bilateral deficit in terms of foreign exchange is with West Germany and already amounts to about 1.2 million each year? To increase its

land force in Western Europe would be financially onerous and would beg the question of just how much share Britain is supposed to take.

There is another area too that needs evaluation at the British level. If the USA were to reduce its commitment to Europe, it follows that the presence of a substantial Royal Naval Fleet in the Atlantic, established to protect both trade routes and reinforcement routes for American troops and supplies in times of European emergency, would itself be in question. This would be ironic. Despite the significant whittling down of numbers of Royal Naval personnel in the last ten years and the consequent gradual redefinition of its strategic role, the Royal Navy has proven its efficacy and value many times over in times of peace and war over the last decade. The campaign in The Falklands could not have succeeded without Royal Naval vessels and crew as prepared and as professional as they were. Moreover, the British presence in the Gulf in the last three years has demonstrated a level of international maritime peace-keeping commitment that stands significantly higher than that of any of its European partners.

Herein lies a larger question still: in an age when British insularity is being eroded in both geographical (with the Channel Tunnel) and political terms, and despite its commitments to Belize, The Falklands, and Hong Kong (until 1997) and, in a less obvious way to the security of the Commonwealth, would Britain still have to show its flag, its prowess, and its presence in the same way if it were to embark on an economic/security policy centred in Europe? If Britain were so involved in the European dimension, surely Europe would have to be less insular itself and look to gaining wider strategic footholds in the Mediterranean and farther afield where so much trouble has been brewing and erupting in recent years?

Strategists are currently arguing that European involvement needs to be intensified on the Graeco-Turkish front, where the Soviets have a possible future gateway into Western Europe, as well as looking at

greater peace-keeping activities in the Middle East, including Iran/Iraq, The Lebanon, Israel, Egypt and Tunisia. To date, the British have been more involved in the Gulf than its European neighbours, despite the fact that the Italians and the French stand to lose most if the stability of the Gulf broke down. The Italians have about the same Gross National Product as Britain and spend half the amount that Britain spends on defence.

Gorbachev and Thatcher

The lead British story in 1989 was Gorbachev's visit, hot from Cuba, to meet the Prime Minister, the Queen, the Lord Mayor of London, 150 factory workers in Watford, and not least, the Very Reverend Michael Payne, Dean of Westminster, at Westminster Abbey. According to Mr Payne, this brief interlude at the Abbey had some effect on the Soviet Premier who remained sombre and respectful as two Soviet military officers in full uniform marched ceremonially to the foot of the Tomb of the Unknown Soldier to lay a wreath. The Dean commented that Premier Gorbachev 'said that he was deeply concerned that politics and morality should go hand in hand and that religion had an important role to play in this'.

This statement, and many other similarly styled ones that helped to establish an all-time high in Anglo-Soviet relations, were typical of Gorbachev's momentous two-day visit and came from the mouths of both the Supreme Commander of the Soviet Presidium himself and Britain's inimitable Prime Minister. Concerning the trials and tribulations of *glasnost* and *perestroika*, she said, 'With all our mind and strength, we want you to succeed . . . with a peaceful revolution'. According to a friend of a friend of an attending VIP at The Guildhall Speech on the morning of the second day, another VIP's wife thought that Mr Gorbachev 'was totally disarming'. But much, as yet, needs to be put to the test.

Back in the Soviet Union, where so much social, and economic upheaval continues to spray-paint the walls of the new decade, the plight of the Jewish Refusniks and the Orthodox Christians, Muslims, Armenians, and

Above: Mrs Thatcher and Mr Gorbachev in London during his visit in 1989. Both leaders continue to have frank, wide-ranging discussions yet adopt a firm line on issues of their own national importance. A matter of weeks after saying goodbye (right), they began the latest round of tit-for-tat 'spy' expulsions.

others (not to mention grey-bearding political dissenters in Siberian labour camps) beg slight questions of Gorbachev's moral and religious fervour. During Gorbachev's visits, the Western public politely overlooked the fact that he is the leader of a superpower whose official policy is institutionalized atheism. Religion apparently is mentioned only on Gorbachev's foreign visits as and when public relations demands that it has to be. The improvement of the Soviet economy remains top of the list of Gorbachev's priorities and, with the alacrity and deftness of a great statesman, he bends all subjects to meet this purpose (this is not to doubt his moral sincerity but politically palatable announcements and private moral feelings do not always sit happily together in one mouth).

Shervardnadze and Howe

As the mutual back-slapping continued between Mrs Thatcher and Mr Gorbachev, the Foreign Ministers, Eduard Shervardnardze and Sir Geoffrey Howe debated matters with less concessionary zeal. Shervardnardze complained bitterly about comments Howe had made in his visit to Pakistan in March when he had urged the Afghan leader, President Najibullah, to step down. According to a Foreign Office source, the Soviet Foreign Minister complained about Howe's statements saying 'it was not sensible to ignore the people inside Afghanistan who had strength and prestige'. Sir Geoffrey, whose own foreign political strength and prestige seems to have grown in the last two years, remained unmoved by this criticism.

Meanwhile . . .

On April 6 and 7 1989, President Bush and his aides were winding up to a fight over news that the Soviet Union has agreed a deal with the Libyans to sell them an undisclosed number of advanced SU24 bombers. At about the same time, the Strategic Defense Initiative Organization, with the blessings of the Bush Administration, was preparing for what turned out to be the highly successful test of a powerful anti-missile laser designed to knock out Soviet missiles in space by deflecting a mega-watt beam by means of huge mirrors mounted on platforms high above the ozone.

The intense beam, which lasted one-fifth of a second during a test run at a secluded valley near San Juan Capistrano, California, was part of a $1.4 billion chemical laser project called Alpha. The Alpha laser is estimated to be eventually capable of producing 2,200 kW of energy.

Mrs Thatcher may have been aware of the import of such exceptionally powerful technology at the time but it did not appear to have entered summit discussions. Perhaps it would not have been diplomatic to mention since Mr Gennady Gerasimov, the spokesman for the Soviet Foreign Ministry, announced that in the summit discussions Mr Gorbachev had asked the Prime Minister to use her influence with President Bush to persuade

him to speed up the disarmament process. Having won a world-applauded public relations exercise in his foreign policy initiatives, the Soviet premier felt himself in a position of strength when indicating that the Americans seemed very slow and rather unclear in their own approach to disarmament issues.

The Libyan jets issue, although pumped and plugged in a hysterical fashion by one or two British newspapers during Gorbachev's visit, elicited no more from the diplomatic lips of the Prime Minister than a statement of regret. Mr Gerasimov was appeasing on the matter, saying that Moscow had supplied kits for no more than six bombers to Libya but their operational range was only 300 miles (480 km) and Tripoli had no refuelling capability. Contentious areas such as these were mostly confined to the Shervardnadze and Howe discussions. Summarizing four hours of initial summit talks at Downing Street, Margaret Thatcher commented that the discussions, which were about world issues, were 'very deep, very wide-ranging, and very friendly'.

Matters in hand and mouth

According to Mr Gerasimov who, immediately after the one-to-one talks between Gorbachev and Thatcher, was briefed about what he could say, the Soviet view married with Thatcher's own. The talks were very friendly and Mr Gorbachev held the British, their opinions and influence in Western politics in very high esteem. Evidently, there was complete agreement on the need to preserve settlement in Namibia.

Gorbachev has been very cautious in his degree of involvement with the Cuban-backed forces in Angola on Namibia's northern border and, by severely reducing financial support for the Cubans, effectively forced their hand in the reduction of Marxist-backed troops in the region. Notably, he and Fidel Castro do not agree on many aspects that concern the enlargement of the fractured communist hegemony around the world.

Thus Namibia, which has since been a thorn in the side of all concerned, helped to kick-start discussions into forward gear last April. In particular, Gorbachev told Thatcher that he approved her position on Namibia and praised her statement on the United Nation's resolution made in the previous month in which she advocated the reduction of UN troops to the region to save them all money. Another useful subject in which Thatcher proved to be a well-versed talker and an attentive listener was that of perestroika or rebuilding. Gorbachev told Thatcher about the achievements, hopes and set-backs of a programme of reform that he envisaged running for many years to come. Thatcher expressed Britain's desire for his success.

The inevitable discussion about the fate of short-range nuclear weapons in Europe was less easy. Gorbachev showed his teeth in preparation for the June summit with President Kohl in West Germany by saying that he considered a programme of modernization of these weapons tantamount to the creation of a new

Left: President Bush – striving to break free of the Reagan shadow and take the initiative from Gorbachev.

class of missile, and therefore an attempt to circumvent the terms of the INF agreement of May and October 1988. Mrs Thatcher, said Mr Gerasimov, 'did not agree with this'.

There was also some disagreement evident about US foreign policy. Gorbachev was said to have expressed concern that the new administration was taking too long to get to grips with foreign policy. Gerasimov, bon viveur and wit, mischievously commented to journalists that some members of the new administration doubtless needed time to learn about an unfamiliar area. Reading between the lines, one might observe that President Bush's vice-presidential experience in foreign policy involved considerable Israeli-Egyptian shuttling and various encounters with the Soviets. Furthermore, as former head of the CIA, there is probably not much the new President of the USA does not know about ticklish foreign political strategies. However, some of Bush's aides may well have needed to bone up on their global geography before making heady plans. Bush merely requires a competent scriptwriter with an eye for the long-term view.

The Soviet opinion, which seems a fair one, is that the momentum in East-West relationships that 'beefed the wellington' during Reagan's latter years should not be lost or slowed. Gorbachev apparently put significant weight on what he believed was Thatcher's possible influence on the new administration. If anyone could unsuspiciously convey the Soviet's good intentions, he thought, she could.

Chemical concern

In these important discussions, Gorbachev did his best to allay Western fears about Soviet stocks of chemical weapons by saying that British experts could make a return visit to the Soviet Union's for further inspections and consultation. About three weeks later, a team of scientists and specialists were invited to go to the Soviet Union for this purpose in June this year, at the same time as Margaret Thatcher's talks in Kiev.

The West's policy on this issue has long been the achievement of a comprehensive, verifiable ban of chemical weapons of all kinds and this includes micro-biological warfare (BW) and chemical warfare (CW) agents. An important event took place in 1988 with the visit of Soviet officials to the Chemical Defence Establishment (CDE) at Porton Down in Wiltshire, England. Since Britain abandoned its own offensive capability in 1959, followed by the USA in 1967, research at the CDE has concentrated on detecting and monitoring the nature, means of weaponizing and the degree of lethality of agents used by various aggressors (notably in the Iran-Iraq War).

CDE is also responsible for the design of protective equipment, such as special respirators and NBC suits, and also devises medical countermeasures, including therapies and prophylactics to treat those who may come under chemical attack. The range and the lethality of potential toxins, nerve and chemical agents is growing and the ability to manufacture synthetic agents from raw chemicals – used for such innocent purposes as agriculture or pharmacy – creates a disturbing profile of potential threat.

Says Mr Graham Pearson, the director of the CDE, 'I personally believe that we have a moral obligation to our fighting servicemen to be able to detect chemical agents, to protect servicemen from their lethal effects and to treat these effects wherever this is humanly possible'. Of all HMG's research establishments, the CDE is, in fact, the only one that is entirely dedicated to protective capability.

In these circumstances, the visit by the Soviet scientists and dignataries must have proved a testing one for Mr Pearson and his colleagues. They have nothing but research excellence to show: nothing to give away and no position from which to step down. The strongest point they could make – with not a little presumption – would have been along the lines that 'if you have the threat, we have the capability to withstand it'. On the Soviet side, however, for the first time since the cold war began, the Soviets actually admitted that they had a stockpile of chemical weapons amounting to some 50,000 tons.

When NATO officials were invited to inspect the

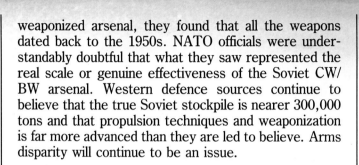

weaponized arsenal, they found that all the weapons dated back to the 1950s. NATO officials were understandably doubtful that what they saw represented the real scale or genuine effectiveness of the Soviet CW/BW arsenal. Western defence sources continue to believe that the true Soviet stockpile is nearer 300,000 tons and that propulsion techniques and weaponization is far more advanced than they are led to believe. Arms disparity will continue to be an issue.

US troubles

As evidenced during 1989, the Americans appeared to spend much more time contemplating their own financial, social and domestic navels than looking for tangles overseas, or engaging in leadership initiatives. Perhaps this introspection is not surprising, given that any new President, especially one paternalistically ushered into place by Pa Reagan, who blazed a trail of glorious public approval on his departure, may think it best to be cautious in establishing his own governing signature.

The Americans had a number of problems to deal with last year which hadn't been apparent as such during the previous Reagan administration. Of major importance, the reasonably friendly, if highly competitive, trade relations that the USA has enjoyed with Japan over a number of years suddenly turned nasty. Almost certainly proving that the cold war between East and West has dissipated, a cross-section of Americans answered a poll about which overseas nation or confederation they thought represented the greatest threat. Japan was rated more of a threat than the Soviet Union. Such a question would not even have been asked only two or three years ago.

The USA's economic relations with Japan deteriorated so fast that a serious diplomatic wrangle became inevitable. The peculiar friendship had its back broken by Washington's decision to rethink its plans to co-develop Japan's new FSX Fighter. Mr Taizo Watanabe commented at the outset that the friction 'was not purely economic. This problem is getting very serious in terms of the political atmosphere in Washington. We can only hope that bilateral problems can be solved without adversarial positions being taken.'

As Japan became more angry and aloof, Washington targeted Tokyo for retaliatory action under a new US Trade Act on the grounds that Tokyo's trade surplus was the product of unfair practices. US hawks such as Mr Lloyd Bentsen, Chairman of the Senate Finance Committee, stated that the USA was 'vulnerable to an economic Pearl Harbor'.

The problem lies with the USA's severe budget and trade deficits which are reckoned to be worsened by its defence commitments in Europe and Asia. American opinion was firm that were the Japanese not so obsessed by exports, they could have alleviated the US deficit by buying US F16 fighter jets 'off the shelf' rather than building their own FXS fighters.

However, as long as there continues the demand in the USA and Europe for semiconductor technology and such new 'telecommuter' products as facsimile machines, it is unlikely that the buoyant Japanese export machine can be controlled by the sale of a few planes. Here can

Below: Infantryman in full Nuclear, Biological and Chemical warfare kit with a Sterling machine gun.

Right: South African troops in Namibia after routing SWAPO fighters while UN forces stood by ineffectually in 1989. In July of that same year came reports of a 'courtesy' visit by imprisoned African leader, Nelson Mandela, to the residence of President Botha. The development was met with cautious responses from the Black community in South Africa. Below: The Palestinian people demonstrate and wait for a solution to their homeland crisis.

please. In his first few months of presidency, he would pop up almost daily at Washington Press Conferences giving an eager and spontaneous account of whatever appeared to be going through his mind. Journalists were – and still remain – bemused by his friendly banter.

Bush was also criticized for his lack of leadership in the event of the terrible Exxon Valdez Alaskan oil slick disaster. After three weeks of trying to clear up the mess, there came a half-page advertisement in national newspapers signed by local businesses and residents. It announced: 'Mr President, we urgently need your presence and personal leadership'. Although it is still too early to make sweeping judgements, such a statement may be levelled at Bush about his want of resolve in foreign political terms.

Mr Bush was visibly more forthcoming in his sympathy and 'leadership' when disaster struck the ancient but highly rated *USS Iowa* last spring with an explosion in the gargantuan gun turret which killed 47 crewmen. This ship, whose captain said 'she is still the most survivable ship in the entire US Fleet', has been in service in one way or another since 1943 and is one of the most impressive and massive warships ever constructed. Re-commissioned and modernized in 1982, *USS Iowa*'s 16-inch (400-mm) guns are still said to knock the whole ship sideways some 10 ft (3 m) when firing a broadside. Its future fate, after a long period of repair, remains undecided.

With Europe in the throes of a weapons modernizing conflict, internal squabbling and dilemma about long-term strategic principles, and with the Americans offering introverted and often paranoiac responses to the rest of the world (while planning further cuts in Defense Department projects to try and ease deficit problems), it was easy for such commentators as Gerasimov at the Kremlin to say of Bush: 'He's trying to be all things to all people.' The inference is that a point in every direction is the same as no point at all.

be seen the real power and rub of economics and how cash balances are far more instrumental in the commencement of hostilities than ideological differences about the distribution of wealth or the democratic versus totalitarian make-up of society.

The U-turn in the Washington decision about the jet fighters was one of a number of zig-zagging decisions that typified the Bush administration in the first year. Within three months of his administration, there were grumbles at home and abroad about Bush's vacillatory style of government. Where Reagan had a totally scripted, well-projected, word-spare and emotionally simple approach to government which fitted the pattern for resolve and steady movement in a definable direction, Bush appeared frantic and too eager to

It would appear that Washington's defence policy as directed by Bush and his Defense Secretary, Richard Cheyney, is to do little more than follow the status quo. There is or has been precious little direction.

However, although Gorbachev is showing a very distinctive policy of openness and friendliness to as many faces as possible (even to the Chinese and the South Africans) is he not also trying to be 'all things to all people'?

The Namibian Independence Process

It was in 1978 that the United Nations Security Council issued policy directive 435 approving the Namibian Independence plan. Only last year after a total of 23 years of war and general strife in the area, did the edicts of the plan begin to be implemented. Never since the Congo, has the United Nations had a more troublesome task than trying to keep apart the crack South African Forces and the straggling but highly determined troops of the South-West African People's Organization (SWAPO). Never was more blood spilt almost as soon as the peace-keeping exercise got underway, and never, it seems, were the hapless UN troops from Finland, Kenya, Malaysia and Britain, less able to cope with the situation.

Unfortunately, key members of the UN, including Mikhail Gorbachev and Margaret Thatcher, were keen to diminish the planned 7,000-strong UN force to 4,650 in order to reduce costs on the eve of the independence programme early last year. SWAPO forces, under the very slack controlling leash of the Angolan Government, were asked to remain in southern Angola, north of the 16th parallel, in order that the UN Transition Assistance Group (UNTAG) could prepare Namibia for elections that were to be held in November 1989.

For reasons best known to themselves, under the leadership of Sam Nujoma (now running 25 years and more), whose people are most likely to win the majority in the elections, SWAPO swarmed into Namibia. The UN force at the time of the incursion numbered a pitiful 900 men and was completely taken by surprise and unable to stop South Africa's much-feared 101 counter-insurgency battalion, complete with sophisticated weapons and armoured vehicles, from rushing into the fray and killing SWAPO forces at the formidable rate of 10:1. the South Africans themselves lost 26 men and had 80 wounded, some seriously.

Armchair criticism is easy, but it is shameful to observe how ineffectual the UN forces are allowed to be when the two sides they are trying to keep apart want each other's blood. One paper reported how a brave 24 year-old British captain of the 30th Signals Regiment tried to oust a dug-in South African platoon section after the carnage was over and the UN forces were trying to lure the mauled guerrillas into UNTAG safe camps. The captain said: 'I don't think what you're doing is correct, sir. Your presence here is not making it easy for us to assemble the guerrillas.' The South African sergeant told him he had orders not to fire but refused to budge.

A UNICEF report concluded that if the Independence programme had gone ahead in 1978, as envisaged, some 10,000 children's lives would have been spared.

The Middle East Settlement

It is going to be interesting this year to see how firm the Americans are in persuading the Israelis to abandon or radically improve their policies of maintaining the Gaza Strip and West Bank – scene of the Palestinian insurrection known as the *infidata* for more than two years. The Soviets, the Americans, the Egyptians, the Jordanians, the British and the Europeans are all endeavouring to settle this question and, in many respects, there seems to be a common accord of purpose, if not of policy.

King Hussain's intervention last year was most notable in pin-pointing one crucial problem. The Hashemite King made it clear that the Israeli's conciliatory (and American-approved) plan, to hold elections in the West Bank and Gaza to choose Palestinian representatives with whom the Israelis could negotiate a settlement, would prove fruitless. He argued that although such a plan may appear acceptable to the fair-minded and distant citizens of the USA and Europe, the PLO would never accept such a plan while the West Bank and Gaza remained under Israeli occupation. The Israelis are caught between the devil and the deep blue sea. They need to cut their force of 10,000 troops tied up in the conflict; they need to be seen to be fair in the eyes of the West and they particularly need the $3 billion that comes from the Americans each year.

Meanwhile, further north . . .

1989 saw the worst violence ever in The Lebanon's war-torn capital. Beirut was virtually under seige for a period of several weeks after the Maronite 'Christian Leader', General Michel Aoun began his 'war of liberation' against the Syrian military presence in Lebanon. Bleakly reflecting the madness of this 15-year civil war, the Syrians themselves apologised to the Soviet Union, who supply most of their armaments, after they fired at a Soviet tug and a divers' support vessel 39 miles (63 km) off the Syrian port of Tautus. Over 130,000 men, women and children have been killed in Beirut since April 13 1975 and as foreign correspondent, Juan Carlos Gumucio, put it at the height of General Aoun's liberating war: 'The country plunged into its 15th year of civil war without a glimmer of hope on the horizon.'

In these and other places around the world, there does seem to be a certain lack of easy, daily civilization. How can people still live and work in Beirut? How can they still live and work in Kabul in Afghanistan, in Tamil territories in Sri Lanka, in Ovamboland in Namibia, in Gaza and the West Bank? The Americans and the Russians continually ask the same questions about those living in Belfast.

Picture Credits

Artwork

The Contributors

BILL GUNSTON was a pilot flying instructor with the RAF. Since leaving the service, he has acted as an adviser to a number of aviation companies. He is an assistant compiler of *Jane's All the World's Aircraft*, and was formerly Technical Editor of *Flight International*.

HUGH LYON has had a lifelong interest in naval matters. After research into the British shipbuilding industry, he has written or co-authored 17 books on navies and warships in the past decade, including *The Encyclopedia of the World's Warships* and the warships section of *The U.S. War Machine*.

MARTIN STREETLY is an aviation and electronic warfare historian who has contributed widely to various military and aviation publications, including *Jane's Defence Weekly* and *Defence* magazine, both as writer and technical illustrator.

CHRISTOPHER DOBSON is a war correspondent and author, winner of the IPC Award of International Journalist of the Year in 1967 for his coverage of the Six-Day War in the Middle East and of the Tet Offensive in Vietnam. He lectures at the Police Staff College, Bramshill, and has written a number of books on terrorism.

IAN HOGG served for 28 years in the Royal Artillery. After retiring in 1972, he became a full-time writer on military subjects, and has since published over 70 books and contributed to defence and military publications throughout the world. He is currently the Editor of *Jane's Infantry Weapons* and *Jane's Military Review*.

DUNCAN BREWER is a freelance journalist with a background in industrial relations, the new technologies and politics. He served with the RAF in Cyprus during the EOKA emergency, and has developed a special interest in the Falklands conflict.

GILES EMERSON was educated at Oxford, and specializes in science and defence-related subjects on a full-time freelance basis; he also writes scripts for radio. He worked for several years with the Central Office of Information, visiting a number of MOD establishments at home and overseas producing publicity and recruitment material.